Happy 1979 John

Film Collecting

Film Collecting

Gerald McKee

South Brunswick and New York: A. S. Barnes & Co.
London: The Tantivy Press

A. S. Barnes & Co. Inc.,
Cranbury,
New Jersey 08512,
USA

The Tantivy Press,
Magdalen House,
136–148 Tooley Street,
London SE1 2TT,
Great Britain

I SBN 0-498-01918-7
L.C. 76-50200

PRINTED IN THE UNITED KINGDOM
by The Halesworth Press, Halesworth, Suffolk

*This book is dedicated to my wife, who put up
patiently with several months of concentrated movie mania.*

Acknowledgements

Preparing this book would not have been possible without the assistance and suggestions of fellow film collectors and other individuals. In particular, I should like to thank the following: John Burgoyne Johnson for the loan of invaluable catalogues, and for showing me unique 17.5mm films in his collection, Maurice Trace for generously sharing the results of his researches, E. O. (Ted) Walker of the Vintage Film Circle for information on the Pathé 28mm Library, Bernard Crouse for the loan of rare catalogues, Brian Coe of the Kodak Museum for information on the Kodascope Library, Paul van Someren for his helpful suggestions and information on Super 8, and the various distributors of films for collectors for their co-operation. I must also express my gratitude to my friend Basil Copper, who persuaded me to write this book, for his help and encouragement.

Contents

Part Six

Part Seven

Introduction

"They don't make 'em like it any more," could be one of the main reasons why people collect old movies. But this is really only a part of the story. People collect films for a variety of reasons. There's the collector who wants films for nostalgic reasons, hoping to capture his lost youth through the magic of the movies. There's the collector building a library of all the great movie classics perhaps to use for a film appreciation teaching programme. There's the film buff who loves all the movies of the past and can find something of interest in anything old on the screen. There's the casual collector who wants a few films to augment the shows he gives of the movies he shot on last summer's vacation. There's the film fanatic who amasses reels in quantity—he just wants a big collection and may never even project his treasures on a screen. And there's the gluttonous collector, an eccentric who's not content with one copy of a film—he has to have several!

Once you catch the movie collecting bug, you could fall into any of the above categories, and this book is intended as a guide whatever your interests. It deals with the background of collecting, the history of the home movie gauges. It covers the true collectors' pieces—and the modern re-prints. And because some technical knowledge of the mechanics of collecting—projection, the handling of film, and the question of photographic quality—is essential for the full interest of the hobby, some information is given . . . in the most straight-forward of terms, I hasten to add.

At the end of the book, after all the surveys of the subjects available on the various gauges, I have dealt with a number of stars and studios—some familiar, some not so well known—who have all provided silent movies of outstanding interest for collectors. This is entitled appropriately "Collectors' Pieces," and gives the opportunity for discussing in greater detail some of the background of the vintage years.

The film industry has never liked collectors and has gone to great lengths to ensure that films do not readily fall into film buffs' hands. It seems strange that in an age when one would have expected a more liberal attitude to the Twentieth Century's most familiar means of visual communication, motion picture copy-right holders—the producers and distributors—have not hit upon a reasonable solution to making prints of classic movies available to collectors. As it is, they seem to have adopted a stance more inclined to encourage piracy of their property rather than its sensible commercial exploitation by direct selling to collectors.

In the past, enthusiasts have collected 35mm movies, and it is from their private collections that the archives of the world have been able to acquire copies of many early films. Even today there are 35mm collectors, dedicated film buffs of the kind whose expertise has helped to unlock the secrets of major producers' film vaults and to recover some of the motion picture classics supposedly lost to posterity. But 35mm movies are outside the scope of the amateur collector. So if you are lucky enough to find a true rarity on the professional gauge it is best to offer it to an official archive, or a collector with facilities to handle 35mm safely. The chances are that the grateful archive—or collector—will get a narrow gauge print made for you to keep in your own collection.

16mm sound is really a library gauge and most 16mm sound prints are handled in the same way as theatrical 35mm prints. They are rented for a certain time, then withdrawn from circulation. They are not sold to collectors. The exceptions in the past (in Britain) have been copies of certain independent productions, generally of little interest for collectors, that have been offered for private sale. But there are still legitimate 16mm prints for sale and these mentioned in the section dealing with Super 8 prints. American collectors are fortunate in having a copyright law which allows movies over twenty-eight years old to enter the Public Domain, providing they have not been re-copyrighted. Even so, since all the major producers re-copyright their movies for a further period of twenty-eight years, most of the legal 16mm prints on offer are from the "independents."

In Britain, the situation is not so clear cut. In fact, as the law stands, some silent movies are strictly speaking in copyright. But there is the compensation that there are producers who have negotiated the rights for the sale of their films on Super 8. The result has been the release of many excellent titles—still in copyright—that can be owned completely legally by collectors for showing in their own homes.

It is only during the past year or two that Super 8 has come of age. Already it is apparent that the effects of the introduction of this new gauge will be more far reaching than that of any of the other home movie gauges to date. Possibly the growth of electronic video recording using cassettes or discs will in time outstrip conventional movie techniques. But the well established motion picture projector is so attractive in its basic simplicity, and its ability to give large screen images easily, it will need video images of movie size on the screen before electronics finally outdates the invention of the Nineteenth Century pioneers. None of this will diminish the enthusiasm for collecting early movies; electronic tape recordings will never supplant reels of motion picture film in the eyes of the dedicated collector.

Finally, a note on tracking down the sources of movies. The reader will find that films are dealt with by gauge, even though some titles have been released on more than one of the collectors' gauges over the years. If a title is detailed under the heading of one gauge, it will not be dealt with under another. The index is designed to be a quick reference to the availability of a title on different gauges, or from several sources. After each title entry, a simple code indicates the source of a movie—past or present.

Part One

All Shapes and Sizes
The Story of the Gauges

Film collecting, particularly of vintage prints of movies, is much concerned with the various film formats that have been introduced through the years, especially the narrow amateur gauges which have been used for the mass production of printed films for libraries and collectors. To put the whole scope of the film material that is to be found by the collector in perspective, this is the story of the gauges.

The basic gauge, the gauge which is used to photograph and project nearly all professional motion pictures, is 35mm. And it is a remarkable fact that not only is 35mm still the standard movie gauge but it is also the oldest. In 1889, Thomas Edison appointed a bright young English assistant, W. K. L. Dickson, to work on the design of a machine that "would do for the eye what the phonograph has done for the ear." There was a good chance that such a machine would be technically feasible. Already other inventors had worked on motion picture devices and had provided some sound basic principles, and the technology of photography—with the invention of dry plates—was sufficiently advanced to enable the fast exposures required to be made. Dickson's experiments led him to the conclusion that for motion pictures to be a success, the individual "frames" would have to be on a flexible transparent base.

It was a piece of good fortune that George Eastman, a photographic plate maker, should have been working on a flexible transparent film for his newly introduced amateur camera, the "Kodak." In 1889, Eastman introduced his Kodak film, consisting of a photographic emulsion coated on a clear plastic base of nitro-cellulose (also known as celluloid or nitrate film). Eastman's conception was soon to revolutionise photography by making it available to the masses with the slogan "you press the button, we do the rest," but the film was to be just as important to Dickson who realised its application to his budding motion picture invention. So Thomas Edison became one of Eastman's first customers for the new celluloid film. Interestingly enough the film was $2\frac{3}{4}$ in. (70mm) in width for the Kodak camera, and Dickson cut it into two equal strips for his experiments—35mm wide!

The design of Edison's movie machine was such that a strip of film had to be transported by sprockets past a magnifying eyepiece. This necessitated perforations or sprocket holes along each edge of the film, and as the film travelled at the high speed of 48 frames per second, four sprocket holes on both

Left, the projector that brought the movies to the world — Lumière's Cinématographe.
Right, Lumière film. Although Lumière used the Edison gauge, perforations consisted of only two circular holes per frame.

sides of each frame were considered desirable. When Edison's motion picture system was introduced to the public as the Kinetoscope in 1893, it used essentially the same film gauge as a modern movie theatre projector.

Although the tiny moving pictures of the peepshow Kinetoscope intrigued the public, who paid their pennies in the Kinetoscope parlours opened to exploit the new marvels from the "Wizard of Menlo Park," the obvious limitations of images that could be viewed only by one person at a time were soon apparent. Oddly, Edison failed to pay the fee necessary to patent his Kinetoscope in European countries, so that it was possible to copy legally these machines in Britain and France. As a result, clever engineers like Robert Paul in Britain were soon manufacturing large numbers of Kinetoscopes for sale to fairground showmen. But Paul was creative, too, and inspired by the Edison invention he designed a projector for the Kinetoscope 35mm films so that they could be enjoyed by audiences just like the familiar "magic" lantern. In France, Louis and Auguste Lumière worked on their own motion picture system, and like Paul they used the 35mm standard, but they did make a slight change to the sprocket hole arrangements, using only two round holes per frame. The Lumière brothers also standardised on a projection speed of 16 frames per second, which proved completely adequate for a well designed camera/projector such as their Cinématographe. And as the Lumières demonstrated their system widely in all the civilised countries, the 35mm width became more familier throughout the world. Actually, the Lumière sprocket holes were soon changed to the Edison standard, thus the 35mm gauge became the most widely used standard for motion pictures within a couple of years of their birth.

A year after 1896, generally accepted as the birthdate of the movies because of the successful projection of films in most large cities in the world, amateur movies were already being advertised. "Animated Photographs in the Home" was the theme of an advertisement for the Watson Motograph, which took "standard gauge films" (already the description standard gauge was being applied to 35mm) with a catalogue of over 1,000 subjects, including *genres* that were going to become familiar screen fare through the years: comic films, sporting films, and war films!

Another notable feature of standard 35mm film was that its nitro-cellulose base was extremely flammable. It got off to a bad reputation in May 1897, when a disastrous fire at a French charity bazaar was apparently started by the film being used at a movie show catching fire. One hundred and eighty people died in the conflagration, many of them members of the French nobility, with the result that there were repercussions in the expansion of the budding motion picture industry in France for the following two or three years. It was not until 1900, that Charles Pathé, for example, was really able to get financial backing to go into production on a business-like scale. And this early disaster together with other cinema fires gave nitrate film a bad name with the public—though usually the major part of the casualties were caused by panic.

Looked at factually, nitrate film is highly flammable. Not only does it catch fire easily but it burns rapidly, giving off gases which are both poisonous and explosive. It can even burn violently without a supply of air and sometimes it can ignite spontaneously. From the film collector's point of view it has another insidious property: it slowly decomposes. First the image fades, the base becomes brittle, and later the film becomes sticky and froths, finally crumbling into a acrid smelling brown powder. Many treasured films have been lost this way, usually caused through storage under incorrect conditions of heat and humidity. With careful control of storage conditions and regular inspection of unstable stock (incidentally, age is not the only cause of deterioration of nitrate film, some batches that were manufactured not long before the changeover to safety film have proved particularly bad in this respect), nitrate film can be kept reasonably well; but this assumes laboratory procedures beyond the scope of the home collector.

On the other hand, safety film—or cellulose acetate film—burns with great difficulty and does not decompose with age. Strangely, despite the trouble with fire precautions demanded by the use of nitrate film in movie theatres, studios, and editing rooms, the film industry preferred to use this dangerous material for over fifty years because of its excellent physical properties (it was easier to splice, had better flexibility, and was less susceptible to wear in the projector than the earlier safety films). Only when new safety films, with better handling characteristics, were introduced around 1950, was the industry finally sold on the new film base. Of course, the minor snags that influenced the film industry over safety film did not really affect the amateur handling of it.

Even the earliest enthusiasts quickly realised that 35mm was too bulky and expensive for domestic use. First in the field with a projector for the home using a gauge narrower than 35mm was Birt Acres. Acres was an inventor and photographer of great resource whose achievements included shooting some of the earliest newsreels and giving the first Royal Command film show, and he has often been overlooked in favour of more colourful personalities without his skill. His home movie system was called the Birtac, a combined camera and projector. This used 17.5mm film—obtained by splitting standard film down the centre—in daylight loading cartridges containing 20 ft. The Birtac cost ten guineas and for an extra two guineas you could have a developing and printing outfit for making positives for projection. For use as a projector, a gas mantle was placed behind a film gate; a dangerous practice since the 17.5mm film was on nitrate stock· However, the optimistic advertisements claimed it was quite safe for home use.

In 1899, the British firm of Wrench advertised their Biokam, another combined camera and projector. Superior in construction to the Birtac, the Biokam also used 17.5mm film, but instead of splitting standard perforated 35mm film, unperforated film was slit and a special perforation punched centrally so that it appeared between the frames—an idea designed to give the maximum area of image and later adopted for 9.5mm. A range of films 25 ft. long, "same duration as films used for public cinematograph entertainments" claimed the advertisements, were available for home shows.

New amateur gauges were also appearing in France. In 1900, Léon Gaumont, one of the greatest French producers before the First World War, marketed his Pocket Chrono, a neat little camera using a centrally perforated film 15mm wide. It was an innovation, being the first movie camera to have a clockwork motor. Another French outfit, the Mirographe, using a film 20mm wide, appeared in the same year. The pioneer director Georges Méliès was associated with the company that marketed this strange movie system whose film had no sprocket holes; notches cut in its side were used to transport it through the camera/projector.

During the next decade, manufacturers dabbled with further amateur movie ideas. Some used 17.5mm with either centre or edge sprocket holes; others devised lightweight 35mm cameras and projectors for home movies. But no one

Left, one of the first projectors for use in the home (1897).
Right, the 17.5mm Biokam camera/projector for amateurs.

was really impressed by any of these early attempts at popularising movies in the home and most of them quickly faded away.

Turning away from the use of reels of film, three unique inventions had an unconventional answer to the quest for the ideal movie entertainer in the home. Realising the gramophone had become the most widely used home entertainer, the Urban Company introduced its motion picture equivalent. In place of film strips, their Spirograph projector used printed film discs bearing a spiral of miniature images. These discs—sold as Motion Picture Records— looked like 10 inch gramophone records, even to the extent of being in the familiar record sleeves. Around the circumference of the discs were perforations; these were used to give the intermittent shift, while the projector head scanned the spiral of pictures. Although a clever idea, the Spirograph, using discs prepared from professional movies, could not be adapted for amateur movie- making, and for an amateur gauge to be successful it was essential that it should be possible to shoot films as well as show them.

Even more unusual, the Oko camera/projector by the Polish inventor

The Spirograph projector and movie disc.

Proszynski, was a kind of movie typewriter. It used a film 12 cm. in width wrapped around a roller of narrow diameter. This film had horizontal rows of 15 small images exposed on it as it moved from left to right behind the lens and shutter. After one row had been exposed, the film shifted up and a row of images was made from right to left.

Last of the blind alleys for the home cinema was the Kinora, a domestic entertainer adaption of the Mutoscope (the flip card movie device that was invented as a competitor to the Kinetoscope after W. K. L. Dickson had left Edison). In this, a reel of paper prints was viewed in a small device not unlike an old-time stereo viewer in appearance. For families, a viewer with several magnifying heads was available. A camera which, unusually, used paper films was sold for the Kinora owner to shoot his own movies. And there was a library—the Kinora Living Picture Library. "This is a collection of lovely child pictures, interesting public events, comedy pictures, sporting subjects, animal studies, and other living pictures which are being eagerly bought up by the Society people," rhapsodised the Kinora copy-writer rather snobbishly. Although there was the proud boast that "Motion pictures viewed in the home with the Kinora are the latest fashionable craze, they rival the gramophone and the player piano as evening amusements," like the Kinetoscope it was doomed because of the lack of a projection system. Today Kinoras have become much sought after collectors' pieces, and at the London auction rooms of Christie's they fetch prices higher than those for more elaborate movie equipment of the past, probably because they can be displayed like any other antique and can be operated by merely turning a handle.

In 1912, the French producer Charles Pathé was the undisputed leader of world film business. He controlled cinemas, manufactured cameras, projectors and film stock, and his studios produced a vast output of films. In addition he sold phonographs to homes throughout the world. Charles Pathé had his

Left, Kinora viewers. Right, a portrait of Charles Pathé.

introduction to the world of entertainment when he and his brother brought an Edison phonograph to attract customers to their bistro at the Place Pigalle in Paris. To the Pathé brothers' astonishment, many a customer wanted to buy their phonograph, so they looked for a machine shop where small phonographs could be made cheaply, and at the turn of the century Pathé's factory was hard pressed to meet the demand for Le Coq, a low price phonograph that provided the famous crowing cockerel symbol, soon to become as well known to movie-goers as MGM's lion as the title trademark for the Pathé newsreel.

Pathé's interest in the movies began in 1894 when he came to London to buy some phonographs, and he left with one of the British imitations of the Kinetoscope as well. He persuaded a French inventor to manufacture Kineto-scopes for him and, when the Lumière projection system proved successful, projectors as well. Encouraged by the popularity of the ambitious productions by Georges Méliès, he built a large studio in Vincennes and began the mass pro-duction of short movies for the mushrooming cinemas of the world. By 1908, Pathé was selling more than three times as many films in the United States as all the American producers together. With a movie empire under his control, Pathé, "the Napoleon of the Cinema" as historian Georges Sadoul has called him, decided to bring movies into the home just as phonographs had brought music. In addition, it would be yet another outlet for the productions cranked out by his studios.

His engineers were given the task of designing a home movie outfit. The result was the first truly satisfactory system for the projection of films in the home. Pathé's engineers were wise enough to base their conception on non-flam film, thus overcoming the public's fears regarding the domestic use of nitrate film. Christened the KOK, Pathé's projector used a brand new gauge: 28mm. This was probably chosen because it could not be economically slit from flammable 35mm stock by the unscrupulous. It used 400 ft. reels, equivalent to 500 ft. of 35mm—a slight economy but not sufficient to make films really cheap.

Also in 1912 the pioneer company of Thomas A. Edison—in whose laboratories the 35mm gauge had been invented—introduced the Home Kinetoscope. The name was the same as the earlier peepshow machine, but it was in fact a portable projector for "Motion pictures for the home, schools, YMCA, clubs, etc." With the co-operation of Eastman Kodak, safety film was supplied for this projector to ensure its acceptance for domestic use. George Eastman himself expressed the view that "the furnishing of cellulose nitrate for such a purpose would be wholly indefensible and reprehensible." The Home Kinetoscope had an ingenious answer for film economy. A film 22mm in width was used, and it carried three sets of images with sprocket holes between them so that a film was run three times through the projector, not unlike a present day multi-track tape recording.

In 1914, the manager of Eastman Kodak's camera works demonstrated a camera/projector system. It used 35mm film that was run twice through the camera rather like the Standard 8 movie system, and it caught the interest of John G. Capstaff of the Eastman Kodak Research Laboratory, who asked to borrow the camera to try out an idea he had for amateur motion pictures. For a couple of years he experimented with a system using reversal processing, in which the film shot in the camera also became the positive for projection. In 1916 his preliminary results were shown to a reluctant George Eastman— dubious because of the failure of the earlier amateur systems. The quality of the images and the possibility of the lowering costs convinced him—and Capstaff was given the go-ahead. Lengthy experiments were carried out to establish the smallest image size to give good quality pictures on the screen. This turned out to be 10mm × 7.5mm, and after the addition of 3mm on each side to accommodate sprocket holes, the result was a film 16mm wide, with 40 frames to the foot. There was a considerable saving in costs compared with 35mm; the reversal process saved the cost of having a positive print made from a negative, and 400 ft. of 16mm had the same running time as 1,000 ft. of 35mm. It was on safety base, of course, and its width had the advantage that it could not be slit economically from 35mm nitrate stock. With America's entry into the war there was a halt in the experiments, so that it was not until July 1923 that 16mm was launched with a camera: the hand-cranked Cine Kodak Model A, and a projector, the motor-driven Kodascope. But the Cine Kodak 16mm system was beaten to the post by Pathé's new amateur gauge 9.5mm.

Even before the First World War, work was started in the Pathé Cinema factory on a smaller gauge for home use than 28mm. The war stopped these

Above, Pathé's 28mm KOK projector.
Below left, 28mm safety film (note the odd arrangement of the sprocket holes).
Below right, Edison's short-lived 28mm Home Kinetoscope gauge.

Left, an unconventional early 16mm projector from Zeiss.
Right, the 9.5mm Pathé Baby projector.

researches but afterwards an ingenious method was devised for the printing of narrow gauge films by reduction from 35mm to give a triple row of images on a special 35mm film stock, and the result was a film 9.5mm wide. Although narrower than 16mm, the frame size was only fractionally smaller, thanks to the use of sprocket holes perforated centrally between the frames. It is interesting to note that although they were invented independently, both 9.5mm and 16mm have 40 frames to the foot—a useful coincidence that was later to make dual gauge projectors possible. 9.5mm was introduced in December 1922 with a projector, the Pathé Baby, and a library of 30 ft. films abbreviated from professional originals in the Pathé repertoire. The compact projector was a hand-cranked machine of unconventional appearance and, unlike the Kodak 16mm outfit which resembled a scaled down 35mm equipment both in its looks and its operation, the Pathé machine was specifically designed to be easy in operation for the unskilled amateur. In fact its cassette loading and automatic threading were in a way pioneering the Instamatic conception of movie-making and projection of more recent times.

Another unique feature of the Pathé 9.5mm system was its notched title device. Instead of using a long length of film to project a title, which in effect was only a still picture, only a couple of frames were needed—a notch cut in the film's edge actuating a de-clutching mechanism in the projector to give a still on the screen. This feature made a considerable saving in film stock, so much so that, although 400 ft. of 9.5mm were nominally equivalent to 1,000 ft. of 35mm, with notched titles 300 ft. of 9.5mm equalled 1,000 ft. of 35mm. A year after the introduction of the Pathé Baby projector, a camera appeared to complete the system, using a reversal process in the manner of 16mm. It is significant that the projector should have a year's start on the camera, for 9.5mm was always to remain the "home cinema" gauge in which film projection was more important than movie-making. During the Twenties an attachment for the projector to enable reels of up to 300 ft. in length to be used, was made available, considerably increasing the scope of the projector. The Pathé Baby system was launched in America as Pathex, but it did not prosper there like 16mm, not having the support of the major film manufacturers. In France and Britain 9.5mm soon had a strong following and was used by many more amateurs than 16mm.

Around 1930, Kodak introduced their Kodatoy projector, a cut-price simple machine more in the spirit of 9.5mm than 16mm. But it was not the real answer to home movies for the millions; 16mm film was still too expensive for a complete breakthrough. Improvements in film emulsions in 1928 made it feasible for Eastman Kodak to look into the idea of a film half the size of 16mm. Even narrower films were contemplated, but in the end the conception of a specially perforated 16mm film that could be run twice through the camera and slit to provide two 8mm strips won the day, primarily because it enabled the same processing equipment to be used as for 16mm. Cameras and projectors for 8mm were introduced in August 1932, and despite the Depression the new gauge made its way. Its popularity was consolidated when in 1935 the excellent Kodachrome colour film was introduced for both 16mm and 8mm.

After Hollywood switched to sound in the late Twenties, the narrow gauges had sooner or later to come to terms with the talkie revolution. In 1929, Eastman Kodak proposed replacing one of the rows of perforations on 16mm with the sound track and, in 1930, R.C.A. manufactured the first 16mm sound projector. Before long, other projectors followed with the Eastman Kodak proposals becoming the standard for 16mm sound. For a while, Pathé did not attempt to bring out a sound version of 9.5mm; instead they introduced a new style 17.5mm gauge on non-flammable base with similar sprocket hole and soundtrack arrangements to 16mm, together with a low priced projector, the Home Talkie. This new gauge had already been used on a semi-professional basis for mobile shows in country districts in France, hence its name Pathé Rural. By 1938, Pathé had worked out a satisfactory format for 9.5mm sound with part of the image area taken to make room for the soundtrack. The results were quite impressive, at their best the equal of 16mm quality at the time. The future for 9.5mm sound was bright, but the Second World War and the invasion of France prevented further developments. On the other hand, the war was a shot in the arm for 16mm which was used in army training, mobile propaganda film shows, education, and the provision of entertainment for service men at active service. Remote out-stations and battle zones were all provided by means of 16mm. And just as the Allies used 16mm, the Germans had their 16mm UFA Schmalfilm. After the war 16mm benefited from experience and improvements brought about by its wartime service, but 9.5mm had to pick up the threads of 1939. And 8mm, backed by the world's leading photographic manufacturers, forged ahead as prosperity returned.

In 1965, the latest and potentially the most important of the amateur gauges was launched by Eastman Kodak. Over the years it had become apparent that the double-eight concept of the original 8mm system was inhibiting the growth of amateur movie-making because of the awkward arrangements of having to lace a film into a camera not once but twice during each run of 50 ft. of 8mm. Also, it was considered appropriate to improve the image area available on 8mm, making it possible for an optical sound track to be accommodated. So the whole of the 8mm concept was re-thought from first principals. The result was a totally new gauge, with no relationship to any earlier gauge other than being 8mm in width. Now just over eleven years later it seems as if the youngest of the gauges has finally eclipsed the remnants of 9.5mm and will soon make Standard 8 obsolete. But one guesses that the professional gauges of 16mm and 35mm will carry on . . .

Looking for Vintage Movies

A Personal View

Collecting movies is rather like collecting paintings. You can buy originals—or you can buy reasonably convincing reproductions. You can track down original prints of films with difficulty, or you can buy—with no trouble at all—one of the Super 8 re-prints that are now the mainstay of the movie collecting scene. It is the original prints that represent the real collectors' pieces, films that were once plentiful, that now require a combination of perseverance and good luck to nose them out. Buying a copy that's readily available may be fun, but to the true collector it is the excitement of discovering a long lost print that gives the zest to movie collecting.

Today, most young collectors begin by buying the usual run of Super 8 "package" movies—cartoons, horrors or comedies—from their local photographic dealer. If they catch the collecting bug they'll soon tire of these standardised re-prints. Their next move is to look for the releases exclusive to the specialised distributors, and after this source is exhausted they will seek out the less accessible movies from abroad. Eventually the true film buff will want to find some of the original prints that were made on 8mm, 9.5mm and 16mm before the Second World War—when the whole idea of home movies was in its infancy. So there is a division of interests in film collecting: on the one hand there are the old prints, on the other Super 8 prints. And although there are collectors who specialise in only original prints, the majority of film buffs have an open mind and will be quite happy to add Super 8 prints to their collection if they are the only source of a film they want.

Leaving aside the element of luck—and there is no doubt that luck has a lot to do with the success in discovering the choice collectors' items—there are a number of more positive ways to track down original old movie prints. Despite the fact that few dealers handle second-hand films these days—most assistants in the photographic shops do not seem to have heard of any other gauge but Super 8 anyway—it is worth haunting the dealers still selling second-hand movie equipment because there is always the chance they may have bought an old projector complete with films in a part exchange deal. There is no doubt that old movies do turn up this way. A trade-in by a church organisation for a new 16mm projector provided one collector with a great rarity. This was a 16mm Western Electric sound on disc projector complete with several movies and their synchronous 16 inch gramophone discs. The prize item was a copy of

The Doomed Battalion (1931), excitingly combining the best of the mountain film style—it featured Luis Trenker, star of several mountain films—with realistically directed First World War action on the snowy peaks of the Austro-Italian border.

Keep an eye on the small ads in the local papers. Some years ago, I saw an advertisement offering a 35mm projector and some films for sale. Although I don't collect 35mm, I couldn't resist having a look at the outfit. It turned out to be a little Debrie projector—the most portable I have ever seen—and pile upon pile of films occupying all the space in the seller's garage. A remarkable find for any 35mm collector.

Another invaluable publication—in Britain—offering a unique market place for collectors and their interests, both for buying and for their wants, is "The Exchange and Mart" (in the current week's number at the time of writing there is a rare 28mm outfit with films for sale). Don't be put off by vague descriptions in these adverts, often submitted by the uninitiated. Once I saw two films described as old-fashioned melodramas. Sight unseen I sent off a cheque, playing the hunch that they might turn out to be something worthwhile. To my delight the hunch paid off. One reel contained two Triangle subjects including an early Gloria Swanson drama *Station Content*, the other reels

Gloria Swanson in Station Content.

contained René Clair's rare attempt at straight melodrama, *La Proie du Vent*. Circulating movie enthusiasts there are the specialist magazines "Movie Maker" and "Film Making," both of which have small ads where films are offered for sale.

In the internationally famous London auction rooms of Christie's and Sotheby's, sales of photographic equipment have become regular events. Movie projectors together with reels of film appear along with the early still cameras, often selling at quite reasonable prices. With the growing interest in the collecting of still photographic apparatus, there's the side effect of people searching their attics for old photographic gear which brings to light projectors and the films that invariably go along with them. At the bottom end of the sales scene there are the fund-raising jumble sales. These are not to be scorned as a source of old films; I know collectors who have found old movies and other cinema memorabilia in the sale at the local church hall.

Another source of vintage movies are the specialised film dealers. These dealers are often collectors themselves, selling films surplus to their requirements to help pay for their hobby, and thus providing one of the main sources a new collector can go to in order to find the films he wants. Some of these dealers are prepared to supply films on approval, returning the prospective purchaser's money if the film does not meet with his requirements providing it is sent back in undamaged condition. Sometimes a nominal fee is charged for viewing the film if it is returned. This does provide some guarantee of satisfaction from both the standpoint of subject matter and physical condition. In fact, collectors are advised to make sure that such an arrangement is possible before parting with any money to an "amateur" dealer.

Like any other field of collecting where rarities in demand are involved, there are the inevitable rogues, people who claim to have certain desirable films, get collectors to send money, then fail to deliver the goods. However keen you may be to get hold of a title, I would recommend checking on the credentials of an unknown source, especially if large sums of money are involved. *Caveat Emptor!*

Similarly, if you decide to advertise a film surplus to your own collection, beware of the apparently enthusiastic buyer who quickly answers your advertisement with a promise to buy, asks you to send the film on, then when he gets your film omits to make payment. Despite constant reminders, such people still avoid parting with their money. The remedy is never to send a film without receiving payment first.

Junk shops have long been a magnet for the movie collector. Over the years I have found the occasional film or two in these shops. For instance, in a local junk dealers I discovered a two reel amber Kodascope print of an Our Gang comedy and several 9.5mm Pathéscope films including some rare shorts on London shot in the Twenties. Here again constant visits are necessary otherwise you'll find some other more persistent movie buff will have beaten

J. Warren Kerrigan in Captain Blood.

you to the post. Even second-hand furniture shops shouldn't be overlooked. Only recently I was tipped off that a downtown furniture store had a 16mm projector. I went along hoping that there would be films with it, but no such luck. Fortunately the projector, an early Kodascope, was a collector's item in its own right.

Look at the sales and wants notice board where you work. From this source I found an old Pathéscope projector and a dozen early notched films. And don't forget to let friends and relatives know about your interest. This can pay off, as happened when a colleague volunteered the information that he had a copy of the Vitagraph spectacular *Captain Blood* that he had no further use for; would I like it? The result was the addition of a print in mint condition to my collection. Never turn down the offer of an old film, amateur or professional, even if it is something you do not want for your own collection. There is always a good chance that there will be someone else who does want it, and you may be able to arrange a swap for the very items you are looking for.

Old movies can turn up in the most surprising places. One strange find I had started with a phone call from a colleague. "You're interested in old films, aren't you? I've got something I think you'd like to see." I called on him and learned that he had found one or two 9.5mm movies in the early closed cassettes on top of a rubbish heap collected together by the keeper at the local park. I figured that there might be more where these odd reels had come from, so the next day I paid a visit to the park's rubbish dump. And there on top of a pile of junk was a cardboard box full of old Pathéscope 30 and 60 ft. films. One spool was a rare newsreel compilation produced by Pathéscope to celebrate the Silver Jubilee of King George V. It was—astonishingly, in view of the fact that it had been out in the open—in such perfect condition that it looked as though it had never been through a projector. The rest of the spools contained amateur movies—usually scorned by collectors—but these were exceptionally interesting, being made as far back as 1926 (the paper band round the circumference of the cassette provided the details). Some were complete films—edited and titled—and others were family records (a well-heeled family judging by the Daimler limousine that featured in these long lost movies).

Incidentally, collectors would be well advised not to turn down offers of amateur movies, particularly those made on 9.5mm and 16mm before the war. When the BFI mounted a special series of programmes about the Thirties, they found the movies which provided the most interesting view of the times were some amateur films discovered in a house awaiting demolition. Well-photographed family holidays and outings can provide a view of life totally missing from the professional output whether it be fiction or documentary. The only puzzle is: why do families dispose of what one would imagine to be priceless records of happy times? Even more alarming is when early movie material is treated as no more than a children's plaything. One collector told me how he found some children in the street playing with short lengths of 28mm film and went hot foot in search of its source, probably a junk heap. And I once found a South Coast secondhand shop selling off odd strips of rare 35mm silent film—taken from full reels—for children to play with.

One strange source of 9.5mm films—and very early items, at that—has been in India. It appears that a photographic dealer in Bombay, the Pathéscope agent for India, had an incredible stock of prints of old films, presumably left over from the days of the British Empire. Many 9.5mm collectors bought films from this firm until recently. The only snag was that the dry atmosphere of India had made some of the copies very brittle.

It is still possible to find 9.5mm movies in the United States. A devoted collector friend tracked down some fascinating films—never released elsewhere—including a couple of publicity reels showing how the family can enjoy film-making and the projection of professional movies in the home using the Pathex 9.5mm system. France is, of course, an obvious place to go for Pathé 9.5mm movies. Some British collectors pay annual visits to Paris to make the rounds of the Flea Market and the photo-dealers to pick up rare items.

But, in the end, finding old movies is largely matter of luck. Pity the poor collector who saw a pile of movies for sale in a London photo-dealer's window.

Just as he was making up his mind to go in and buy them—a hand appeared and removed the reels from the window. Someone had got there first. . . .

Are vintage movies a good investment? Will they, like original early photographs, rise dramatically in value? Present indications are that there has been a reasonable appreciation in the price of original movie prints: a rare notched 9.5mm reel bought in first class conditions a decade ago for £3 could fetch as much as £9 today. Much the same applies to 9.5mm sound and 16mm movies, though amber Standard 8 copies are sometimes found at the same price as second-hand modern Super 8 prints. Attempts to jack up the cost of vintage film prints by certain individuals have been resisted by collectors. After all, film is a fragile and perishable commodity and an indifferent dupe on Super 8 may be preferable to a damaged—and possibly unprojectable—16mm print of superior pictorial quality. On the whole, prices asked by reputable dealers for second-hand 9.5mm and 16mm prints in reasonable condition represent good value. The prices obtained for vintage movies have yet to match the inflated figures that have been obtained for early photographs. But with the increased interest in old movies, the laws of supply and demand are slowly beginning to bite. Examples in good condition are already starting to appreciate considerably.

Points on Print Quality

To the collector of films, print quality is as important as good road performance is for the car enthusiast or the perfect reproduction of sound is for the hi-fi expert. Even the more casual collector, occasionally projecting a silent comedy to supplement his own attempts at movie-making, is unhappy if the quality of the package movie he buys compare badly with his own efforts. Unfortunately, the dismal clips of silent movies used on TV and the low standard of some 8mm prints give little idea of the beautiful photographic quality that was an ingredient of the silent cinema. So here let us take a look at some of the characteristics of silent film photography, and the methods used to translate these images on to the collectors' gauges.

Right at the beginnings of the cinema the men who photographed the earliest films had the great traditions of the work of the Victorian masters of the still camera to aspire to. Even though the basic equipment chiefly responsible for setting the cinema age in motion—Lumière's Cinématographe—was rudimentary, it was accurate and well engineered. Films still in existence shot on this pioneer camera/projector are not only remarkably steady but have gradation and print quality equal to the late Victorian standards of still photography. Collectors interested in the earliest era of the silent movies can buy excellent Super 8 copies of a selection of the films that formed part of the original Lumière programme of late 1895, including the legendary *Train Entering a Station* and *L'Arroseur Arosé*, the first glimmering of screen comedy. Compared with Super 8 prints of much more modern films, the quality of these Lumière re-prints is first class; they are certainly worth the attention of any collector building up a comprehensive archive.

During the first decade of this century the rise of inventive skilled cameramen like D. W. Griffith's associate Billy Bitzer, who adapted the lighting and compositional techniques of the still photographers, gave the movie camera a creative role bringing dramatic overtones to scenes that would have been impossible if it had been set up merely as a recording machine. Other cameramen in the pre-First World War years inspired by Bitzer's work on D. W. Griffith's Biograph one-reelers imitated some of his techniques like, for example, the attractive back lighting of exterior shots.

The introduction of the finely engineered Bell and Howell camera in 1912 revolutionised camera design, and this equipment was to be used on the majority of Hollywood movies until the introduction of sound. Whatever Hollywood movies might lack in the story department, their standards of cinematography were generally excellent. On the continent cinematography was given a status in advance of Hollywood. The superb luminous photography of J. Julius on Swedish classics like *The Atonement of Gosta Berling*, Léonce Burel's stunningly vigorous images in Abel Gance's *La Roue*, and Eduard Tissé's compositional power and precision on *Battleship Potemkin* were camera artistry at its peak. The country that more than any other gave power to the cameraman was Germany. Karl Freund, one of the most creative of all cinematographers, who put his stamp on many German classics, was instrumental in freeing the camera from its fixed tripod, using the crane, flying camera, and dolley for powerful dramatic effect. As an inventor and creator of ways of moving his camera about a studio set, together with a fine control of lighting, Freund was without peer. As a lighting cameraman with an ability to create glowing, living portraits of the players in expressionist dramas (superior to Freund in this field), Fritz Arno Wagner was another German camera master. In Britain, Jack Cox, who

Top left, Mary Johnson in The House of Arne, *photographed by Julius. Top right, Severin Mars and Ivy Close in* La Roue, *photographed by Burel. Below, superimposition in* Vaudeville *and montage in* Metropolis, *both photographed by Karl Freund.*

formed a productive association with Hitchcock, was doing fine work in the silent days. But generally British silent film photography, left in the hands of uninspired cinematographers, was flat and lifeless, so that German cameramen enticed to the new BIP studio in Elstree in the late Twenties were treated like visiting royalty. It is interesting to note that, when the German Theodor Sparkuhl was brought over to photograph *The Flying Scotsman*, he came with his personal camera outfit and lenses.

Until 1925 the main film stock used by Hollywood cameramen was Eastman Standard Negative. Although sometimes inaccurately described as ortho-chromatic or ortho-stock (i.e., sensitive to blue and yellow), this widely used material was in fact only blue sensitive, distorting the rendering of coloured objects in terms of black and white. In particular, blue sensitive stock was not kind to the human face. To highlight the all-important eyes and mouth, corrective make-up was used to counteract the distortion given by the stock. But the gums—which could not be made up—photographed very dark thereby accentuating the teeth. Pale blue eyes photographed badly; Eastman Standard stock was much more flattering to brown and dark blue eyes, hence the success of stars with these valuable attributes. With a speed of only 25 ASA, Eastman Standard's insensitivity to normal artificial light made it essential to use lamps that were rich in ultra violet to illuminate indoor sets. A side effect from the use of these lamps was a painful form of eye inflammation; Klieg eye, as it was called after the most widely used arc lamps, was an occupational hazard for any busy actor in the early days of studio-made movies. Despite these disadvantages, the high acutance (the ability to record fine detail), coupled with the deep focus of the small aperture lenses of the time, gave images of distinctive clarity. After 1925, panchromatic film (i.e., sensitive to all colours including red), originally introduced for early colour processes by Eastman Kodak, began to come into use for normal black and white cinematography. The result was change in the "look" of silent movies: the hard edge of blue sensitive stock gave way to the softer gradation of "pan." Panchromatic film with its red sensitivity made it possible to use tungsten studio lamps instead of the old arc lamps but, being less powerful, wide aperture lenses were needed. This in turn made the deep-focus effects of the early Twenties hard to achieve; fuzzy background to close-ups became a fashionable feature of the talkie Thirties. It was not until Orson Welles's cameraman Gregg Toland experimented with fast panchromatic films and small aperture lenses for *Citizen Kane* that deep focus came back into vogue again.

All this adds up to the fact that the standards of photography in silent movies was of a high order. So for the full enjoyment of this essential ingredient it is important that the quality of these images should be preserved in any reprints. In view of this fundamental aspect, it is helpful to understand how these prints were made in the past, and how present-day Super 8 prints are produced.

Original silent 35mm prints were printed by contact from the master

Above, mass production in the Edison Studios, circa 1912.
Below, shooting a movie in the mid-Twenties (from Merton of the Movies).

Two cameras were often used in the silent days, one to provide a duplicate negative.

negative made in the camera. Usually when a second negative was needed by a Hollywood producer for the British and European market, a second camera shot a negative in parallel alongside the main camera (duplicating techniques for preparing a dupe master negative were not fully perfected until the talkie era). All the professional films available to collectors began their life on 35mm, narrow gauge prints being made by optical reduction from the 35mm originals.

An economical printing system was used for producing 9.5mm reduction prints. From the original 35mm negative a fine grain duplicating positive was printed by contact. This special positive was then reduced in size optically to give three 9.5mm negatives on a specially perforated 35mm stock (the perforations were narrower than usual to allow for the three 9.5mm strips). Release prints were contact printed from this triple negative and finally the film was slit into three 9.5mm bands and the outer pilot sprocket holes discarded. This system had the further advantage that it was possible to use 35mm equipment for the processing of these films. The results could be excellent and early 9.5mm prints, whether they be 30 ft. shorts or 300 ft. reels, are of invariably good quality. They accurately reflected the 35mm originals from which they were prepared. Some early 9.5mm prints have a warm tone image, adding considerably to their charm and giving them a unique vintage patina. 9.5mm prints of the Twenties and early Thirties were of course made at a time when it was possible to have access to the

The Pathé 9.5mm triple printer and (below) a triple 9.5mm band before slitting.

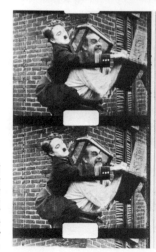

The best known of all collectors' movies, Easy Street, *seen in a direct comparison of an early Pathé 9.5mm "notched" print and a Kodascope Notice that both frames have excellent definition.*

A frame from a Standard 8 "amber" print (The Indians Are Coming), *showing the remarkably high quality.*

master 35mm negatives of the films selected for release, so their printing got off to a good start.

After the Second World War the standard of the British made prints dropped and they lacked the sparkle of the earlier Pathéscope output. The original triple master negatives from which they were printed had become worn and it was no longer possible to get access to the 35mm originals, though prints being made by the parent company of Pathé of France were still excellent.

Prints from the 35mm silent movies that provided the subjects for the Kodascope library and the Cine Kodagraph package movie shorts were reduced to 16mm by Kodak in their own laboratories. Original 35mm master negatives were used to print two 16mm positives at a time (processed as separate films) in one reduction step, and it is this one step reproduction that led to the excellence of these Kodak prints. At their best they resembled original 35mm theatrical prints in quality. The distinctive feature of these Kodak prints was that they were invariably printed on amber tinted film stock (actually this was a film stock with a base tint varying from lemon yellow to pale orange). Although originally called "Sunshine" stock by Kodak, prints made on it are popularly known as "amber" prints by collectors. The reasons for the use of this stock are obscure— possibly it was because it would instantly identify Kodak prints and discourage illegal duping while it also had the advantage that it masked some of the minor blemishes in printing that might appear on the screen.

Like the 16mm prints, the 8mm Kodascope Library films and Cine Kodagraphs were printed on amber stock in the laboratories of Kodak. These 8mm prints were printed by direct reduction from the 35mm master negatives, two at a time on 16mm. After processing, the film was slit into two 8mm strips in the same system used for the films shot in a Standard 8 movie camera. Once again the print quality was outstanding, largely due to the direct reduction from 35mm negatives. Some of the Kodak 8mm prints on amber stock are the best ever to be printed on the narrowest gauge.

A final thought on amber print stock. It had the advantage of giving a pleasant brightness and warmth to the screen image, ideally suiting the comedies and outdoor action pictures that predominated on the Kodascope Library's output. One feels it would have been less well suited to the more sombre European subjects that were so much a part of the Pathéscope archive.

Even to the non-technically minded it will be obvious that if you can make a positive print from a negative, so you can make a negative from a positive print, and hence from it further positive copies. Unfortunately there is a price to pay for this practise—known as duping—and that is a loss of picture quality; every time a photographic image goes through a reproduction process there is a loss of definition and gradation. The simplest method of duplicating a 16mm film is to have a reversal duplicate made. This is done by making a contact print on a special film which can be reversal processed rather like the film in an amateur movie camera. Carefully done, with attention to the correct exposure, such copies can be remarkably good, even if they forfeit some of the subtleties of the images in the original. Over the years 16mm dupes have been made from existing amber prints; many of these are disappointing, though, usually because they have been printed without the correct "grading" needed to bring out the best in the copy.

Because of the fine tolerances involved in getting worthwhile duplicate copies from existing prints on 8mm, the cost of having a satisfactory 8mm dupe made is often more expensive than 16mm copying, and only in exceptional cases is it worth considering. Although there have been 9.5mm duplicating services available, very few dupes have been made on the gauge from original 9.5mm vintage releases, though there are some 8mm prints available that have been made successfully by reduction from 9.5mm originals, of a quality satisfactory by normal 8mm standards. It will be apparent that duping—especially by the reversal process—is the method used by film pirates to make illicit copies from 16mm library prints. Modern duplicating stocks, using a simplified processing procedure, have made the production of dupes relatively easy, but the standard of prints offered by such dubious sources is likely to be low, quite apart from the illegality of owning such copies.

With the resurgence of interest in silent movies in the Sixties and the drying up of the supply of new 9.5mm and 16mm prints of old films, a new source of prints sufficient to satisfy the demands of the growing numbers of collectors was needed. The answer was 8mm, which had already outstretched the competing pioneer gauges as the favourite amateur movie-making medium. Fresh copies were made on the smallest gauge by reduction from existing prints of silent movie classics. But the slow production techniques used by Kodak to make their beautiful amber prints were no longer considered to be economically viable by the laboratories, many of which were now equipped to handle 8mm reduction printing. In place of the old method, a faster, more cost-conscious system is operated. From a 35mm or 16mm positive—ideally a special positive made on a fine grain duplicating film—a master "double-eight" 16mm negative is made by optical reduction. This negative, bearing two rows of images, is then used to produce double-eight contact prints on a continuously running printing machine. After processing, the film is slit to give two 8mm prints for projection.

Theoretically there is no reason why Standard 8 prints made by modern laboratories should not be acceptable for projection in the home on a screen of moderate size. While many of the 8mm prints have been satisfactory, there are unfortunately other prints that suffer from poor definition and gradation and there are several reasons for this. As it is now well over forty years since the last professional silent film was made, it is virtually impossible to find original 35mm negatives to work from, as was the case in the heyday of Kodascope and Pathéscope. Sometimes 35mm projection prints are used with good results, but more often the tendency is to employ 16mm prints as pre-print masters. And when these are well-worn projection prints, scratched and full of splices, or dupes from material of low standard, the final 8mm reproductions are unacceptable. If on the other hand a Kodascope 16mm amber print is used as a master, the 8mm results can be excellent. Another reason for bad 8mm prints is the incorrect exposure and processing of the double-eight inter-negative. This shows in the final print as images that are excessively grainy, or lacking highlight or shadow detail. In fact the quality of 8mm prints is very dependent on the skill and care of the operator making the inter-negative. There is nothing so frustrating as getting a print of classic film where it is impossible to follow the action because of the above faults, most of which could have been avoided if the inter-negative were correctly made.

Since Super 8 has now become the basic collector's gauge, there have been several developments in the production of prints. Some Super 8 prints are now made as many as four at a time in parallel rows on a special 35mm film, and there have been useful benefits in the use of a "wet-gate" for printing the inter-negatives. Using this technique the pre-print master travels through a liquid which effectively fills all the scratches in a worn film while it is being exposed on the negative. Generally, Super 8 prints in black and white from silent movies are being made to a better standard than the average 8mm releases of the past. But it is essential that collectors should be vigilant about inferior prints; they should reject copies that fail to give a decent picture on the screen. Reputable distributors of Super 8 films will investigate such complaints and replace poor copies with acceptable material. This chapter has been primarily concerned with the print quality of silent movies, but exactly the same principles apply to Super 8 sound films. It might be thought that prints from sound movies, being made from more up to date pre-print material, would automatically be better in quality. But this is regrettably often far from the case, and mute and sound prints from talkies can be as bad as prints from silent movies, most of the faults stemming from the use of worn pre-print material and badly graded inter-negatives. Ironically, there are better Super 8 prints of Lumière's original programme of 1895 than those of some sound movies made in the last couple of decades.

With the growing interest in colour, laboratories are giving extra attention to the special requirements of Super 8 colour prints. Colour printing involves all the problems associated with black and white—and then some. Without getting involved in technicalities, it should be mentioned that the use of a special pre-print master, the production of the double—or quadruple—eight inter-negative using one of the correct film stocks, is essential if good colour quality is to be maintained. Remarkable improvements in Super 8 colour prints have been made in the last couple of years, and work is continuing on new developments. One promising technique being used is to make each print a direct reduction from a 35mm master negative, in effect a return to the original Kodascope system. Now that sound colour prints on Super 8 are being sold in ever increasing numbers the laboratories are at last taking the new gauge seriously.

Part Two

Pathé's 28mm KOK

1912, when Scott made his ill-fated expedition to the South Pole and magician Méliès made a movie spoof of it, and D. W. Griffith directed his first epic *The Massacre*, was the year Charles Pathé introduced his new 28mm safety gauge for home and non-theatrical movie shows. The key feature of this new conception of movie presentation was a projector called the Pathé KOK. The name was a kind of pun on the French word "coq" meaning cockerel, the famous trade-mark of the Pathé organisation. (On reflection, an interesting choice of name since it was not unlike a shorthand version of "Kodak," the word invented by George Eastman for easy pronunciation internationally.) Apart from handling the new gauge, the KOK was unique in other respects. It was reasonably portable, completely independent of mains electricity, gas or oil lamps (forms of illumination already used on portable 35mm projectors) as it had its own generator, and it had a compact optical system with an excellent lens. It looked, when it was in its carrying case—handsomely decorated with a transfer of the Pathé "Coq"—just like a sewing machine. It was not surprising that the designers of a precision machine for use in the home should have been inspired by the Singer sewing machine, which at this time was probably the only piece of accurate machinery in common domestic use.

After its introduction in France, the 28mm projector was put on sale in Britain by Pathéscope Ltd., a company set up to sell the new machine and the range of Pathétone gramophones. To provide the necessary films for the projector called the Pathéscope in Britain, the company opened a comprehensive library of films at their Piccadilly offices. These movies were released on 400 ft. spools, most of the subjects specially edited for the new format with the standardised titles that were later to become a feature of 9.5mm. As the titles were translated into several language versions, a standardised printed type was essential.

One of the most popular of the later releases on 28mm was the multi-part version of the famous Pearl White "serial" *The Perils of Pauline* (actually this pioneer "serial" was less like the cliff-hangers that were to come later than a modern TV series with each episode more or less self contained). It is, in fact, only through 28mm that copies of this historic movie exist today; all the available 16mm and 8mm versions have been reduction printed from the original 28mm releases. This is the reason for the peculier subtitles in the available prints of *The Perils of Pauline*. Like all the 28mm versions, the titles were in the standardised Pathé type with the film's original titles translated into French, then these French titles were re-translated back into English. The result of this backwards

translation was some strange, totally un-American titles completely out of
spirit with the original film and, worse, sometimes ludicrously illiterate.

The subjects on the 28mm gauge in the comprehensive catalogue issued by
Pathéscope after the library was well established during the First World War
were wide ranging in their scope. There were the usual educational items, an
aspect of the gauge clearly important to Pathé, with such titles as *The Water
Beetle*, *Gathering Lemons in Sicily* and *Catching Crocodiles* anticipating the many
similar subjects that were to be released later on 9.5mm. There was the inevitable
Life of Christ, always a money spinner for Charles Pathé, whose various episodes
in this series made between 1908–1914 were issued in eight reels on 28mm.
Bringing the catalogue up to date were several wartime newsreel subjects:
The European War, *Kitchener's Army*, and *Life of a French Soldier at the Front*.
Anticipating the future pattern of narrow gauge releases, the 28mm user was well
supplied with comedy. There was the outstanding work of the great French
comedian Max Linder (one of Pathé's most popular players) with titles including
Max as a Gymnast, *Max as a Chiropodist*, *Max Learns to Skate*, all selected from
the incredible output of this prolific comedian from the cinema's infacy whose
talent was even acknowledged as an influence by Chaplin. A number of shorts

The 28mm repertoire was rich in movie records of music hall acts.

featured the comic with the turned-up nose, Charles Prince, called Rigadin in France and Wiffles in the English 28mm releases: *Wiffles at the Telephone*, *Wiffles Is too Clever*, and *Constable Wiffles*. There were multi-reel dramas like *In the Grip of Alcohol* (yet another of the early silent moralisings on demon drink), Albert Capelliani's *Two Orphans* (an early try at the subject Griffith was to use for *Orphans of the Storm*), and his *Notre Dame de Paris*. Later the comedy department was to be expanded with movies starring Harold Lloyd in his early comic guise of Lonesome Luke, with Snub Pollard, and Bebe Daniels (subjects that were theatrically released by Pathé Exchange in the States).

It was not only in Britain and France that the KOK and 28mm were to make an impression. In America, a civil engineer with faith in the educational value of the movies was looking for a system that did not use flammable 35mm film (already discredited for causing fatal fires). He was Willard Beach Cook, who registered the Pathéscope trade mark in America in 1913. At first he organised the production of the Pathé KOK using imported parts, but before long was selling an all-American machine with refinements of his own design. By 1918 there were one hundred of the "Popular" model in use in New York City schools, and in the same year the motion picture engineer Alexander Victor developed a simple 28mm projector—the Victor Safety Cinema—enthusiastically proclaiming its merits in comparison with the competing 35mm De Vry portable machine.

28mm led the field in America for the next four years, its value underlined by the S.M.P.E. recognition of the gauge as the standard for all non-theatrical shows. Willard Beach Cook organised a lending and sale library of 28mm movies, and his first catalogue of Pathéscope 28mm releases listed 935 titles— represented by over 1200 reels. There were plenty of educational subjects, but Cook was equally concerned that the library should provide entertainments as well as information. So an important section of the American Pathéscope library was devoted to "De Luxe Specials" feature-length movies starring Charles Chaplin (even the comparatively rare *Shoulder Arms*), William S. Hart, Douglas Fairbanks, Mary Pickford, Charles Ray, Billie Burke and other silent film favourites.

The American 28mm library flourished until the introduction of 16mm by Kodak in 1923. Despite the fact that there were claimed to be 10,000 28mm projectors in use at the time, the library was disbanded in 1924, the first victim of competition from the new safety gauge sponsored by the world's most powerful photographic manufacturer. Willard Cook's valuable expertise at operating a successful film library was not lost, though. Kodak were shrewd enough to take him on to run the Kodascope Library when it opened in 1924, and it was his flair that built up this 16mm library into a unique cross-section of the American silent cinema. He remained in charge until it was finally closed in 1939.

On the face of it, it might seem a rather fruitless pursuit even to consider the possibility of collecting 28mm movies. No films have been issued since the mid-

Twenties, and when they were released they never received the attention given to the other amateur movie gauges. But 28mm films are still being discovered, their very rarity acting as a challenge to some collectors; it is rumoured that there is a collector in France with over 1,000 reels of 28mm. Oddly, it is easier to find the Pathé KOK projector than the films. Many of these well engineered machines still exist in good condition, and those that are found have often been the property of social clubs and churches—an indication that they were too expensive for individuals to buy during their heyday. Handling 28mm can be a problem, though, with films that are found having become brittle and shrunken with age so that they fail to run smoothly through the projector, resulting in further film damage. With the low-powered lamp available, the light on the screen is barely adequate, although the inventively-minded collector might be able to adapt these machines to more up-to-date standards of lighting. It is also worthwhile considering the addition of a motor to drive this basically hand-cranked machine.

For all its snags, 28mm is undoubtedly a true collector's gauge with many treasures to be found—films that no longer exist in any other form. With only a small reduction from 35mm, the picture quality of these copies is virtually identical with that given by an original 35mm print and, because 28mm acetate film is stable, it will have survived where unstable 35mm nitrate copies have perished.

Pathé's Ill-Fated 17.5mm Format

It was a Saturday in the autumn of 1963 at the mellow lecture theatre of the Royal Society of Arts, a not-to-be-missed occasion for movie collectors. Pianist Arthur Dulay, doyen of silent film piano accompanists, was to provide the musical background—and many well known personalities from the world of the cinema had made a date to come. The reason for this special event was the first showing in Britain for many years of a reasonably complete version of Abel Gance's astounding silent film *Napoleon*. Even more remarkable, the rare copy of this film was on a gauge scarcely known to most movie buffs—it was Pathé 17.5mm.

17.5mm, as we have seen, was often used in some early attempts at an early amateur movie system. Even though Pathé in France had had a good measure of success with their 9.5mm gauge, they were looking for a format with more professional potential to be used with portable equipment for mobile filmshows in country areas where there was no permanent 35mm cinema. Appropriately called Pathé Rural, the newly designed 17.5mm gauge—obviously inspired by 16mm—squeezed the maximum advantage out of each frame by having the sprocket holes actually encroaching on the picture area. A mask with radiussed corners in the projector gate prevented the sprocket holes from appearing on the screen: the result was a picture format not unlike that on a TV tube. This new format went into use for mobile cinemas in France in the late Twenties but was not heard of in Britain until the spring of 1932 when a sturdy silent projector, the Rex, was advertised for the first time. Far more interesting to collectors, though, were the films made available for the 17.5mm projector owner in the Rex Library organised by Pathéscope. Once again a film on the life of Christ seemed all important in the launching of a new Pathé gauge, so there was an Italian religious epic, *Christus*. Actually, this 1912 Italian version of the New Testament directed by Alberto Pasquali was, considering its age, quite an impressive movie having more in common with the Italian spectacles of the time like *Cabiria* than the earlier French Pathé versions of the story with their primitive look resembling animated Sunday school lantern lectures. The same film in much abbreviated form was also released on 9.5mm.

Oddly, considering that Abel Gance's magnificent *Napoleon* was in the same programme of releases, there was Henri Roussel's tepid, lifeless look at Napoleon, *Destiny* (1925), in seven reels (the same movie also appeared on 9.5mm in three reels and has frustrated collectors by having a title so easily confused with Fritz Lang's *Destiny*). Both *Christus* and *Destiny* are in private collectors' hands and whatever they may lack in cinematic appeal there is no

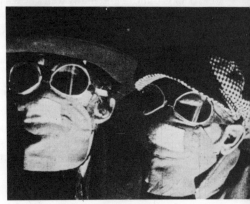

Above, Albert Dieudonné as Napoléon *in Gance's epic. Top right,* The Promised Land *with Raquel Meller. Right,* Belphegor – a *serial released on 17.5mm and 9.5mm in feature versions.*

doubt about their outstanding picture quality and the way in which they preserve the essentials of original 35mm prints with their tinted sequences and completeness of their footage. Even more desirable from the collector's point of view are the copies of the outstanding French silents, Henri Roussel's thoughtful—and powerful—look at the racial prejudice in *The Promised Land* (1925) and Raymond Bernard's spectacular *The Chess Player* (1926) with its exquisitely macabre finale; but so far prints of these two movies have failed to surface. Other collectable titles that surely must exist somewhere are the French serial of the Twenties, Desfontaine's *Belphegor* (1928), in fifteen reels (the British 9.5mm version is only two reels in length, the French eight reels) and Britain's brightest silent star, Betty Balfour, in *Betty's Chance*. The most desirable, and most important, of all the 17.5mm silent releases was the fine seventeen reel version of Abel Gance's *Napoleon* which, with its tinted and toned sequences, the excellence of its print quality, and its running time of $4\frac{1}{4}$ hours, must be one of the versions nearest to Gance's original conception. A print of this rarity is in the collection of a doctor living in East Anglia, and it was this copy that was shown at the Royal Society of Arts' show. Strangely enough, it was bought from an ordinary photographic dealer.

In Britain, 17.5mm is best remembered as the gauge that made possible the first breakthrough into home talkies at a reasonable price. The Pathéscope 17.5mm Home Talkie, costing £60 when it was first introduced in the autumn of 1934, was cheaper than anything comparable for 16mm. Contemporary movie magazines were not totally impressed, considering that the introduction of another film gauge so like 16mm was hardly necessary (the new 17.5mm sound format had the sound track occupying the space normally carrying one of the rows of sprocket holes in the same way as 16mm film) and hoped that Pathéscope would soon adapt their new projector for 16mm sound—already, at this time, established as the narrow gauge sound standard in Britain and America.

Pathéscope backed up their new 17.5mm projector with a comprehensive library of titles, the first list of subjects being issued in January 1935. At the time, the films were only available for hire—there were no outright sales. Subjects selected were mainly from the movies theatrically distributed by Pathé Pictures Ltd., like *The Sphinx* (1933), a murder mystery with Lionel Atwill as a murderer with an almost perfect alibi, and *Speed Brent Wins* with western star Bob Steele, both produced by Monogram, leader of Hollywood's Poverty Row B picture outfits. From Britain came BIP programmers starring light comedians from London's theatreland: Claude Hulbert in the frothy *Heads We Go* (1933) and Stanley Lupino in a traditional bedroom farce, *Sleepless Nights* (1932). There were also obscure American independent movies like the coal mining drama

Left, 17.5mm sound film. Right, Gracie Fields in Sing As We Go – *typical fare for the 17.5mm talkie projector owner.*

Fury Below (1935), a subject rarely touched on by Hollywood's major studios, with silent picture hero Rex Lease as a talkie B picture supporting player.

More interesting as collector's material were two of the immensely popular films made by Gracie Fields for Basil Dean at Ealing Studios in 1934. Overlooked in its time, *Sing As We Go* can now be seen as an authentic picture of the cotton mill workers in Lancashire at work and play in the Depression years of the Thirties, climaxed with "Our Gracie" leading the triumphant mill girls back to work singing the film's stirring title song. *Love, Life and Laughter* updates the story of Nell Gwynn, with Gracie as the orange seller making good in society. It has one hilarious encounter between the irrepressible girl from Rochdale and Robb Wilton as a magistrate in his famous music hall *persona* of Mr. Muddlecombe, J.P.

There is also a spy yarn from BIP starring Norwegian Greta Nissen, *On Secret Service* (1934), ably directed by Arthur Woods, maker of a number of extremely effective thrillers before his death in the Second World War robbed the British cinema of a potentially leading directorial talent. One director to go to Oscar winning heights was Carol Reed whose prentice movies, *It Happened in Paris* (1934), a romantic comedy with John Loder, and *Midshipman Easy* (1935), starring a very youthful Hughie Green in the name part, appeared on 17.5mm. In addition, there were numerous shorts culled from the vast output of Pathé Pictorials and Pathétones, pioneers of the bland "full supporting programme" *genre*. It's a measure of the triviality of these reels that one edition featured women's hat fashions inspired by the Abyssinian War but failed to mention anything about the trail of death in this Thirties' disaster. The main interest in these "variety" shorts today is the radio and music hall acts invariably used to round off each edition. Somehow the flat photography with an immovable camera aptly complements the awfulness of some of these acts, though often the Pathé Pictorial performances are all that survives of once popular variety stars.

Despite the proud boast by Pathéscope that in France there were 4,823 theatres equipped with Pathéscope 17.5mm talkie projectors, showing a total of 54 million feet of film per week, 17.5mm disappeared in Britain as suddenly as it arrived. The last release made in April 1939, and there was no further mention of the gauge by its sponsors. The library was sold off in 1941 to the Wardour Street firm of Illustra Enterprises who in turn sold the films to collectors. It is from this source that those 17.5mm films circulating today came onto the market. Like 28mm, 17.5mm is very much a specialist collector's gauge, with all that it implies in the challenge of tracking down worthwhile subjects.

Kodascope and Others
The Sources of 16mm Vintage Films

"A cinema in your own home! Your own moving pictures—the boys setting up new records—the girls at tennis—the children filmed without knowing it! Fascinating living pictures you can show in your own living room, and as clear and flickerless as you get at an up-to-date cinema . . . In addition to showing pictures of your own making, you can hire pictures from the Kodascope Lending Library—pictures showing all the favourites—Tom Mix, Valentino, Norma Talmadge etc . . . Doesn't that sound like a jolly thing to bring into your home?"

It was on this appealing note that Kodak put out one of their earliest advertisements for their new 16mm gauge for amateur movies. Like Pathé, Kodak had designed their new gauge to be both a means for amateur photographers to shoot their own movies, and a medium of home entertainment using professionally made films. The original 16mm outfit consisted of the Cine Kodak A camera, a bulky hand-cranked machine, and its companion projector, the Kodascope model A, a cumbersome machine rather like a scaled down professional projector but capable of providing an excellent facility for projection in the home or at school. To back up the use of the projector as an entertainer, Kodak opened the Kodascope Library of 16mm movies with a wide ranging catalogue of subjects.

By the spring of 1925, the Kodascope Library, under the expert leadership of Willard Beach Cook, late of the Pathéscope 28mm Library, was fully operative in both America and Britain. It was an instant success with the lucky owners of a 16mm outfit, and we find in the Kodak Trade News of 1926 the following testimonial from a happy customer: "I would like to add that my first experience with the Kodascope exceeds anything I had anticipated. I personally prefer the Kodascope to the ordinary cinema as the films are as good and steady as in an ordinary cinematograph theatre. Being able to show pictures in one's own home with incidental music provided by the BBC is better than anything you can get in a cinema theatre." Already the public was only too aware of the shortcomings of the cinema when it came to sound. Most cinemas could only afford a piano but the home showman could have a BBC orchestra electronically amplified. Altogether, this letter seems to anticipate TV in the home.

To the collector of 16mm movies, the Kodascope Library is of considerable importance. As we shall see, it has been the source of many movies that have been found and preserved in amateur archives, and it has also been the most

important source of master material from which to print the many modern
Standard and Super 8 reproductions of silent films that have been released.

The full scope of this remarkable library can be found in the pages of the
bulky catalogue of 1931 when it was in its heyday. There were major listings of
films in eight categories—Education, Travel, Sport, Manners and Customs;
Industries and Agriculture; Popular Science; Useful Arts and Natural History;
Comedies and Juveniles; Reconstructed and Modern History; Animated Cartoon
Comedies; and Dramas. With refreshing frankness, the library let one into the
reasons for the different pricings of films on hire; they were the royalties paid to
the producer, story value, the photographic quality, the prominence of stars,
the cost of reproduction, and comparative length. Although some of these
factors are fairly obvious, it is interesting that picture quality was a factor in
deciding the value of a film. If only some modern distributors of 8mm movies
could be so honest with their public! In fact, as mentioned elsewhere, the quality
of many Kodascope Library prints was excellent, as much care being taken in
their printing as with theatrical release prints on 35mm. There was also a warning
for hirers who kept a film too long: "The profits of a film library depend upon
the continuous earnings of its films. An idle film not only makes no profit, but
it deteriorates in value from age and changes in public taste." (If only the mana-
gers of the Kodascope Library had known that these old movies, far from
deteriorating in value, have done just the opposite!)

Looking briefly at the non-fictional sections of the library of 1931, the range
covered was not dissimilar to the selections of Pathé 9.5mm 30 ft. subjects, with
titles like *Hydro-Electric Power in the Southern Appalachians* to *The Birth of an
Aeroplane* (by courtesy of the Fairey Aviation Company Ltd.). British imperialism
got a boost in the five-reel *British Birthright*, concerning a special service squadron
of the Royal Navy that was sent to show the flag in the principal parts of the
Empire. Of especial interest to present day collectors is *A Movie Trip through
Filmland*, and there were even movies shot by amateur Cine Kodak camera
owners at Brockland car races. Even more collectable are the early silent editions
of the long running Screen Snapshots series when it was produced by CBC
(Cohn, Brandt and Cohn), a company rather rudely nicknamed Corned Beef
and Cabbage before it changed to Columbia and carried on the S.S. (Screen
Snapshots) series right up to modern times. These cheaply made movies featured
movie stars in their off-screen moments and proved that even the professionals
could be just as silly in front of the camera as any amateur moviemaker's
family. Within the lists of numerous travel subjects there were two travelogues
by the British pioneer Cecil M. Hepworth. One of these, *A Day with the Gypsies*
(c1910), ingeniously has the camera playing first person as a stranger on the
gypsy scene and features some quite brilliant photography: in a pulled-focus
shot, a gypsy comes right up to the camera for a big close-up of two frothing
mugs of ale, in a tracking shot along the hilly road there are views of stunning
stereoscopic quality. There is also much in evidence Hepworth's idiosyncrasy for

beginning and ending each shot with a quick fade rather than a straight cut, a technique that probably stemmed from his experience as a magic lantern operator in the late Victorian era. The Hepworth fades work rather well in this movie, which has the added interest of preserving a picture of the English landscape before the car took over. This is, of course, one of the pleasures of collecting non-fiction films; the chance to see unspoilt countryside and towns before "development" is both nostalgic and fascinating. There were also travel movies by that early movie explorer, Martin Johnson, a real life Carl Denham who brought back scenes of the wild never seen before by Western man.

Already in the early listings there were the Chaplin Mutuals (see Part Four). Otherwise, many of the comedies were forgettable. There were important comedies, though, like the series made by Larry Semon for Vitagraph in the early Twenties with Oliver Hardy, before he teamed with Stan Laurel, as the heavy. Of these, *The Sawmill* (1922) is one of the best to modern eyes; the catalogue says "Thinness of plot is more than compensated for in variety and speed of action." There was also an excellent batch of comedies from Fox including *The Tennis Wizard* (1927): "A society comedy in which the very ignorance of the hero causes his unexpected success in winning the championship game against the really superior skill of his opponent. A summer resort environment showing the 'idle rich' at play, and particularly the younger set in which the girls are greatly in the majority. Rather subtle situations instead of the usual slapstick style." Thus says the catalogue, but, in fact, this is a superbly photographed comedy with a sunny, carefree atmosphere that somehow revives the Twenties as we imagine they were. The pace is fast, and the gags that are built around a tennis match—not a particularly promising comedy subject—are delightfully inventive. The little known Earle Foxe is a dapper "silly ass" hero with a fine sense of timing. One of the sexiest comedies—again from Fox—was appropriately *Girls* (1927). In this, a bashful freshman is chased around the campus by a number of cute co-eds out to educate the virginal hero. When he gets a "soul kiss" from pretty Sally Phipps, he's really switched on and the girls cannot get away from

Left, preserving the rural scene: Hepworth's A Day with the Gypsies.
Right, Earle Foxe in The Tennis Wizard.

him. The coy eroticism of this comedy reminds one of the Busby Berkeley brand of humour a few years later. Using one of the most enjoyable gag ideas of silent comedy, the "surprise reversal" (a scene is completely different to the way it appears at first sight), the Fox two-reeler *Light Wines and Bearded Ladies* (1927), again with boisterous Sally Phipps, starts with a scene of what appears to be graduation day at a university but which is in fact barbers getting their diplomas at a school of hairdressing. The action takes on a crazy turn when Sally and the hero operate an airborne barber's salon, where customers lose their hair and gain beards with cheerful abandon.

The true measure of an archive must be judged by the quality and scope of the dramatic features it contains, and there is no doubt that the Kodascope Library had a number of important silent features. But when one looks into just what was available—taking into account the riches that were produced during the Twenties—the range is surprisingly restricted. Of the major studios' productions, movies from Universal predominated. There were several features from Paramount and a few from Warner Brothers and First National. But there was nothing from D. W. Griffith, and only a couple of Continental films of the period. Just as today, major studios are chary about releasing their productions for collectors other than in abridged form on Super 8; so, in the Kodascope era, M-G-M, the Goldwyn Company, and United Artists never allowed their films to reach 16mm. And even though he made his films for Paramount, none of the most famous silent movies of Cecil B. De Mille were issued by Kodascope, though some of the movies produced by his own company—but not directed by him—did reach the home screen. Because of this lop-sided range of features, Kodascope's range did not include films with Mary Pickford, Lillian Gish, Greta Garbo, John Gilbert, Ramon Novarro, or Douglas Fairbanks (except in the very early *The Americano*, 1916), though there are Wallace Beery, Reginald Denny (well represented by several of his light-hearted comedy features) and his charming co-star Laura La Plante, Colleen Moore in her famous Hollywood story *Ella Cinders* (1925), Richard Barthelmess in the college drama *The Drop Kick* (1927), and Mae Marsh, Constance Talmadge, Norma Talmadge, Dorothy Gish, Mary Astor, Rudolph Valentino, John Barrymore, Charles Ray, and Norma Shearer, all represented by some of their lesser films before they became stars. There is another point about the Kodascope features. Contrary to the belief of some collectors, many of these releases were cut, often to the standardised length of five 400 ft. reels.

Important Kodascope feature releases—many of which are still now widely available thanks to Standard and Super 8 re-prints—include the following. Lon Chaney was to be found in *The Shock* (1923) which is little more than a Universal programmer of no particular merit other than to see this remarkable actor in action. There was also the famous, over-rated *Hunchback of Notre Dame* which was released in a full version of ten reels complete with colour tinting—red for fire scenes, blue for night scenes, etc., in exact reproduction of the 35mm theatre

Left, *Sally Phipps in* Light Wines and Bearded Ladies. *Below centre*, *Douglas Fairbanks and Carl Stockdale in* The Americano. *Far left*, *Pauline Frederick as the "older woman" in* Smouldering Fires. *Right*, *Lon Chaney in* The Shock

original. Once again the main reason for enduring interest in this Universal blockbuster of 1923 is Chaney; by any standards his performance defies the test of time and remains moving and disturbingly grotesque—a plea for sympathy and pity for the disabled. But when Chaney is not on the screen the result is a stodgy spectacle acted out by an uninspiring supporting cast, and it simply does not chime with Hugo's powerful original.

That fine director Clarence Brown was represented by two of his best silents, both Universal; *Smouldering Fires* (1925) with Laura La Plante and Pauline Frederick, and the subtly characterised *The Goose Woman* (1925) with Louise Dresser. By releasing *Merry Go Round* (1922), Kodascope paid at least a partial tribute to Erich von Stroheim (it is, of course, the film he was taken off part way through by Irving Thalberg, then production head at Universal, and completed by Rupert Julian largely to von Stroheim's original script). But why did Kodascope never release *Foolish Wives* or *Blind Husbands* (both directed by von Stroheim for Universal)? Ernst Lubitsch was represented by his witty version of *Lady Windermere's Fan* (1925), made for Warners with an excellent early part for the polished Ronald Colman. Interestingly, Kodascope also issued *One Arabian Night* (*Sumurun*) (1920), the elaborate fantasy Lubitsch made in his German days, which starred both the exotic Pola Negri and himself as the hunchback, one of the few Continental subjects to get on to 16mm in Britain and America. The other German films to get released by Kodascope were the famous version of *Othello* by Dimitri Buchowetski with Emil Jannings and Werner Krauss, and *Volga Volga* (directed by V. Tourjansky in 1928), a powerful movie well photographed by Franz Planer and starring Hans von Schlettow and British actress Lillian Hall-Davis. American directors of merit were represented by Monta Bell's delightful romance *King on Main Street* (1925) with Bessie Love and Adolphe Menjou, suave and cynical. In not dissimilar vein there was Mal St. Clair's *Grand Duchess and the Waiter* (1925), and his highly regarded *Are Parents People?* (1925). Richard Dix starred in Frank Tuttle's fast-moving motor racing drama *The Lucky Devil* (1925), and there were James Cruze's *The Covered Wagon* (1923), now completely ordinary but in its time regarded as the first Western epic, and the actionful *The Pony Express* (1925) (almost a sequel). In the realms of high adventure, there was *Grass* (1925) the remarkable documentary by Ernest B. Schoedsack and Merian C. Cooper on the semi-annual migration of a remote Persian tribe. This movie was one of the earliest attempts by a major studio to sell a factual subject to the movie-going public used only to synthetic thrills. But there were some completely synthetic thrills in *The Lost World* (1925), based on Conan Doyle's fantasy adventure story, starring Wallace Beery as Professor Challenger. With its special effects by Willis O'Brien, this was virtually the silent blue-print for *King Kong* (1933), coincidentally produced and directed by Schoedsack and Cooper.

Raoul Walsh is represented by the uncharacteristic *The Wanderer* (1925), more in the mould of De Mille than Walsh. There is lavish spectacle when the

Left, Willis O'Brien's pioneer animation of prehistoric monsters in The Lost World.
Right, Wallace Beery as Professor Challenger.

pagan city is destroyed in the midst of a great feast to Ishtar, with special effects given the full tinting treatment by Kodascope. A two reel version called *The Feast of Ishtar* was also released of this major Paramount feature starring Ernest Torrence, Wallace Beery and the seductive Greta Nissen as a priestess of Ishtar.

By 1938, some of the earliest features had been withdrawn, but generally that year represents the Kodascope archive at its peak. Compensating for the loss of the American features, there were several interesting additions from the British cinema of the late Twenties. These included a batch of titles from the new British Lion studios at Beaconsfield which had concentrated at its beginning on Edgar Wallace subjects (Wallace was one of the directors of the newly-founded company). *The Clue of the New Pin* (1929), with the attractive Benita Hume and John Gielgud as the effete murderer was released in its full eight reels. This film, incidentally, was one of the first British sound films—released with added dialogue after the silent version had been completed. And *The Ringer, The Flying Squad* and *The Forger* all provided rather stodgy movie versions of Wallace's sensational crime novels. Much better was Gainsborough's *The Crooked Billet* (1929) with Gordon Harker and the blonde, beautiful Madeleine Carroll, directed with humour and pace by Adrian Brunel, one of the strange, equivocal figures of the British cinema, a man who always seemed to be on the verge of something great but never made it. His variable output also included the incredibly tepid *A Light Woman* (1928), again with Benita Hume but novelet-tish and lifeless in its action. Graham Cutts's *The Triumph of the Rat* (1926)—also for Gainsborough—had that great figure of the British stage, Ivor Novello, as the Rat, a totally improbable character of a romantic *apache* in the French

Underworld. Somehow Novello's too perfect looks did not suit the cinema and he wisely concentrated on the stage, though he did make the excellent *The Lodger* (1926) for Hitchcock. Gainsborough brought over the German director Geza von Bolvary to make the railway thriller *The Wrecker*, with first rate photography by Otto Kanturek. This melodrama of 1929 written by Arnold Ridley, with Benita Hume, the American Joseph Striker (who had appeared in *The King of Kings* as John the Disciple), and the Hollywood star, now on the downgrade, Carlyle Blackwell, was climaxed by a train smash and the producers were able to persuade the Southern Railway to smash up a real locomotive for the accident. Unfortunately the director liked the crash so much he repeated it—from different angles for several smashes throughout the film—and it was all too obvious. There was inept continuity, the editor failing to observe the most elementary rules of screen movement with the result that the suspenseful build-up to the crashes was chaotic rather than thrilling. Because of its nostalgic look at the great days of steam railways it's a film of perennial fascination for collectors who are also steam railway buffs. Miles Mander's excellent comedy of manners *The First Born* (1928) featuring Madeleine Carroll and John Loder, one of the few British movies of the late silent era to get at least one cheer from the critic Paul Rotha

An attractive feature of Kodascope prints is that they invariably retain the original titles. Here is a selection of main titles.

Rin Tin Tin.

at a time when British movies were considered the most backward on the screen, remained in the catalogue for a while, as did some of the British International Pictures productions, represented by Dupont's excellent *Piccadilly* (see part 4) and others. These were the peak of British movies—albeit dominated by German talent—to reach 16mm.

The movies of the most famous of all dog stars were given particular attention by Kodascope. Known as mortgage lifters by the hard pressed and small time Warner Brothers' outfit of the mid-Twenties, the Rin Tin Tin melodramas were—and still are—great fun. Beautifully photographed on carefully selected locations, they are Hollywood programmers at their best. Titles that appeared were *The Hills of Kentucky*, *Where the North Begins*, *The Night Cry*, *The Clash of the Wolves*, and *The Lighthouse by the Sea*.

Looked at now, the real strength of the Kodascope Library at its prime in 1938 was in the remarkable cross-section of American short comedies that were available. Apart from the regrettable non-appearance of Buster Keaton, virtually all the other major—and minor—comedians were handsomely represented. It has, incidentally, been one of the major disappointments of movie collectors that so few of Buster Keaton's comedies have appeared on the collectors' gauges.

This loss has been partially redressed in recent years on Standard and Super 8, but even now there are many of his finest films that are outside the grasp of the collector. The curious copyright arrangements that seemed to have dogged his brilliant films over the years has been a disaster for connoisseurs of film comedy. Chaplin's lack of ownership of his Mutual comedies may have represented a considerable financial loss to the great comedian, but the wide coverage these comedies have enjoyed down the years has ensured the lasting popularity of Chaplin even when the later features under his control were out of the public eye. Indirectly they probably helped build the legend that brought the public flocking to the cinemas to see the later Chaplin features. In comparison, Keaton's comedies have had little exposure on the screens of the world since their original release; and now his work appears to be carefully rationed in its appearances, always under the auspices of the present owner of the jealously guarded copyrights of some of his best loved films. Oddly enough, several of Keaton's lesser known shorts were released on 9.5mm in France before the war.

Chaplin is strongly represented by almost all his movies for Essanay and Mutual (see part 4) in prints that are complete with their original titles. Harold Lloyd was covered by a well chosen cross-section of some of his best shorts made when he was still closely allied to Hal Roach. *Spring Fever* (1918) with its action all on location in Griffith Park, and *Just Neighbours* (1918) with its pleasant suburban setting and more or less friendly rivalry between Harold and his early partner Snub Pollard, are typical of the free-wheeling, happy, little comedies of Lloyd's "Rolin" comedy period. A vast improvement on the crudities of his Lonesome Luke character (rather obnoxious to modern eyes), these comedies with the original team from the early days, Bebe Daniels and Snub Pollard, are almost the precursors of TV situation comedy. *Captain Kidd's Kids* (1919) returns to the earlier knockabout, but with considerably more production value. In this Harold has a wild party before his wedding day, and his mother-in-law breaks off the engagement and takes daughter Bebe to the Canary Islands. Harold has a dream in which the mother-in-law is a pirate chief with Bebe Daniels as the prettiest of her all-girl crew. His films seemed to improve when he had as his partner Mildred Davis (selected after Harold saw her in *Marriage à la Carte* with Bryant Washburne—a movie incidentally released on 16mm in Britain after the war). Bebe Daniels was an excellent comedienne in her own right, but probably too strong a personality as a mere foil to another comic. *From Hand to Mouth* (1919) was the first of the Harold Lloyd comedies to feature Mildred Davis. It has Harold as a down-and-out befriending a little girl and her dog. He saves Mildred from being kidnapped by Snub Pollard as a comic villain. There's a wonderful chase with dozens of cops that Harold manages to alert by committing a minor crime in front of them till he's chased by the whole force—a gag not dissimilar to the one Keaton uses in a completely different way in *Cops*. *Haunted Spooks* (1920) is a standard "spook" comedy; a mini *Cat and the Canary* in fact, with Mildred inheriting a ghostly mansion providing she and Harold live

Frames from Never Weaken, *one of the first – and one of the best – "thrill" comedies.*

there for not less than one year. The inevitable crooked solicitor tries to do her out of the money with a whole range of "frighteners." There are some haunted house gags too in *I Do* (1921), though for the most part this is a completely realistic domestic comedy with Harold having a terrible time looking after a mischievous boy and a baby. A brilliant pantomimic set-piece with Harold trying to fit a teat on the baby's bottle already marks him out as one of the great comic talents of the silent screen. Best remembered of all is *Never Weaken* (1921), a thrill comedy with all the essentials of Lloyd's later work.

The films of Laurel and Hardy that reached the Kodascope Library were scarcely typical of the work of this well loved pair of clowns. All from the year 1927 when Hal Roach was releasing through Pathé, they show the comedians before they were really teamed together. In *Love 'Em and Weep*, Stan Laurel is called in to prevent an old flame of Jimmy Finlayson's from pestering him. Stan makes his usual bungling attempt at covering up the trouble—and the film ends with Stan sitting on Jimmy's shoulders in a kind of double drag act. Oliver Hardy only has a small supporting role as the judge invited to Finlayson's home. Not particularly funny, this film was re-made as *Chickens Come Home* in 1931

The beginnings of a team:
Do Detectives Think?

with Hardy in the Finlayson role. An anachronistic Stone Age setting is an unusual background for Stan and Ollie trying to get wives in *Flying Elephants*, interesting in being a type of subject they never repeated. In *With Love and Hisses*, Stan goes for a rather camp line in humour that was ditched when the team finally integrated. *Sailors Beware* has Laurel as a taxi driver and Hardy as a ship's purser being fooled by some crooks including midget Harry Earles. The only subject in this batch which bears any resemblance to the Laurel and Hardy team to come was *Do Detectives Think?* where they are a couple of incompetent detectives employed to act as bodyguards to Judge Jimmy Finlayson whose life is threatened by the homicidal brute Noah Young just escaped from jail. Already the team's pieces of business are to be found in incidents like their bowlers getting mixed up, being frightened by their shadows in a graveyard, and the chase around the house where they are terrorised by the murderer (quite a realistic portrayal for a comedy). It is with this film that the team of Laurel and Hardy is first seen, but they were to make more films before they were completely integrated. Even here Stan still has his hair slicked down—the springy brush was to come later.

Harry Langdon was covered in a batch of the enjoyable two reelers he made for Mack Sennett. There was *His First Flame* (1927): Harry's fireman uncle wins his sweetheart from him and Harry has to make do with the girl's sister. *Boobs in the Wood* (1924) has shy Harry working at a lumber camp, bullied by the foreman, and helping to capture a wanted outlaw. Meeting up with an old wartime buddy whom he finds burgling a theatre—this is the mainspring of *All Night Long* (1924) which also features some hilarious action in the trenches in the First World War. There is more conventional comedy when Harry gets mixed up with a Chinese tong war while doing his duties as a crossing sweeper in *Feet of Mud* (1924). *Saturday Afternoon* (1926) is splendid with henpecked Harry joining a workmate for an afternoon out with a couple of girls on the make. Harry ends up in the rumble seat: "just a crumb in the seedcake of life," the subtitle goes.

*Charley Chase meets Fay
Wray in* Isn't Life Terrible?

That tantalisingly inconsistent comedian Charley Chase appeared in a few titles. Full of interest is *Isn't Life Terrible?* (1927) with Charley as a fountain pen salesman winning an ocean liner trip. It uses the long flight of steps that Laurel and Hardy pushed a piano up in *The Music Box* for one of its scenes, it has a very young Fay Wray in a small part, and it finishes with a wildly funny sequence on a truly appalling old tub of a liner. A generous sampling of some of the fine comedies made by Mack Sennett for Pathé in the Twenties include the work of that bouncy, clever little comic Billy Bevan. *Lizzies of the Field* with rival garage proprietors in a 250 mile road race for a big prize has Billy in his finest hour battling it out with Andy Clyde. This one reel of uninhibited smash-ups and automobile violence is so jam-packed with crazy car action that it's been used more than any other Sennett film for TV clips and inserts. No doubt they all stemmed from Kodascope Library prints.

Kodascope was good on cartoon series. Max Fleischer's ingenious, imaginative *Out of the Inkwell* in which a real life Max was combined with the adventure of his cartoon character Koko (he also turns up in the later Fleischer talkie Betty Boop shorts) was covered with about twenty titles. Bud Fisher's pioneering cartoons of his newspaper strip of Mutt and Jeff appeared, together with a batch of pre-Mickey Mouse Walt Disney Oswald the Rabbit subjects. But the best represented of all the silent cartoon stars was Felix the Cat who appeared in over forty reels animated by the prolific Australian cartoonist Pat Sullivan. To complete the animated cartoon scene, Kodascope had a few of Paul Terry's Aesop's Fables and Ub Iwerks' Flip the Frog. (Iwerks, an animator of Dutch parentage was, of course, the originator and animator of Mickey Mouse for Walt Disney. Flip, not improbably, bears a close resemblance to the famous mouse.)

Take a bunch of talent kids and put them into situations any child would love to be in and you have Hal Roach's formula for Our Gang, a series that ran through several generations of children, spanning the Twenties silent era right

Right, Pat Sullivan's Felix. Below left, Bud Fisher's Mutt and Jeff. Below right, Max Fleischer's Koko (Out of the Inkwell).

I HAVENT EATEN FOR SO·LONG·THAT IF I ATE AN OLIVE IT WOULD SHOW

up to the talkie Thirties and Forties. The original silent team of freckle-faced Mickey Daniels, fat boy Joe Cobb, blonde Mary Kornman, and best known of all, the coloured boy Allen Hoskins who played the little black girl Farina, were undoubtedly the best. Twenty-five of their inventive comedies directed by Robert McGowan were featured by Kodascope and they are invariably fresh and entertaining even though their world in which children made their own fun seems totally to have gone. *Firefighters* where they build a fire engine out of a bootleggers still and *One Wild Ride* with Farina getting a crazy ride in a home-made taxi (one horse power—the horse pushes!) are typical.

Meanwhile over at Universal City in 1926, Carl Laemmle built his own university campus on the studio backlot in an early attempt to appeal to the teenage audience. Universal's Calford was the scene of the *Collegians* series of two reelers, each featuring a sporting climax with popular freshman George Lewis and sneaky rival Eddie Phillips battling for the honours. Kodascope released nearly twenty of these likeable movies reviving the Jazz Age with their students in zig-zag patterned sweaters, their open-topped tourers, and pretty flappers. Three years later Universal returned to the teenage scene with the

Sporting Youth series, this time centred on the adventures of a tomboyish girl and her friends in a small town.

Although the Kodascope Library was the most important source of silent movies in the Thirties, it was not the only one. In Britain there was the Ensign Library. The long-established company of Houghton Butcher Ltd. aspired to be a comprehensive supplier of cameras, projectors, and services, so it was only natural that they should have organised a library for the benefit of the owners of their range of clumsy Ensign projectors. The library was quite enterprising and boasted a number of outstanding titles that had eluded Kodascope. In addition Ensign had the 16mm rights of the Walt Disney Mickey Mouse and Silly Symphony subjects—alas only in silent form. These were generally sold outright on 100 ft. reels—called Ensignareels, rather like the package movie shorts of today.

Like Kodascope, the Ensign Library had a good coverage of comedy shorts for hire. Some were exclusive to Ensign, for example *Moonshine* with Lloyd Hamilton, a tall comedian with frog-like features and a funny walk. This fast, crazy comedy directed by Charley Chase is one of the few silent comedies using Prohibition as a mainspring for humour that actually manages to be very funny. Hamilton's *Dynamite* has inventive fun in a munitions factory with a chicken that drinks nitro-glycerine and lays exploding eggs! There was an excellent batch of comedies made by the English comic Walter Forde in the early Twenties. Imitative of the American style, with Walter himself often borrowing the gestures of Chaplin and Lloyd, they are usually enjoyable with well-timed gags and the added interest of being shot on location in suburban streets near London. *Walter's Paying Policy* is one of the best: a *tour de force* with the comic as an insurance salesman trying to steal a vase to prove the value of insurance to its owner and getting mixed up with a burglar. Away from comedy there were the *Dick Turpin* shorts, with the highwayman (played by Kenneth McLaglen) photographed in the unspoilt countryside of Kent, and the cinematic cases of *Sexton Blake* (a cut-price Sherlock Holmes imitator). All Walter Forde's full-length comedies which he both directed and starred in

Walter Forde, Britain's leading silent comic.
Right, a typical Forde gag: mixing up the posters.

were also available from Ensign, including the excellent spy thriller spoof *Would You Believe It?* (1929) and Forde's switch from comedy to straight direction in the detective drama *The Silent House* (1929). Chaplin's first attempts at movies longer than the two reel format, *Shoulder Arms* (1918) and *A Dog's Life* (1919), appeared in complete versions (surprisingly, in view of the incomplete dupes that have been subsequently released). Ensign also provided a full version of *The White Hell of Pitz Palu* (1930), the great mountaineering romance directed by G. W. Pabst and Arnold Fanck, and featuring Leni Riefenstahl and the German air ace Ernst Udet.

Another major British library was operated by the leading photographic dealer Wallace Heaton, whose catalogue supplied surprising riches. There were copies to be hired of *Waxworks* (1924), with Conrad Veidt, Emil Jannings and Werner Krauss; *Warning Shadows* (1922), Artur Robison's expressionist masterpiece with Fritz Kortner; and Eisenstein's epics—*Battleship Potemkin* (1925) and *The General Line* (1929). Of these titles, Wallace Heaton's proudly proclaimed, "Wherever you try in this country we are certain you would not find a selection nearly as good as ours." In the States, Bell and Howell operated the Filmo Library. "All the famous comedians of the silent screen, plus the incorporeal heroes of the comic strip, are now at your service. Take them home and let them amuse you and your loved ones," said the Chicago firm in 1938. There was also "a world of travel and of nature—brought to your fireside by the Filmo Library—a world encyclopaedia in pictured motion."

It was a feature of the Kodascope Library that none of the titles were offered for sale but were only available on hire. To redress this situation, Kodak introduced their Cine Kodagraphs (Cinegraphs in the States). "Just as you collect worthwhile books for your library, so, as the owner of a home movie projector, you will want to build up a collection of interesting films," suggested the 1939 catalogue of Kodagraphs. But in fact the selection was not particularly inviting, there was no comparison with the riches that the opposition, Pathéscope, had for outright sale. The subjects were familiar extracts with Charlie Chaplin, Laurel and Hardy, Our Gang, Charley Chase, and a dozen Felix cartoons (Felix seems to have been the mainstay of early package movies). There was also a generous helping of documentaries ranging from travel items to newsreels. They were, of course, extracts from films in the Kodascope Library. Cine Kodagraphs do turn up occasionally and, despite their abbreviated footage (the maximum length was 100 ft. of 16mm), they have some interest for collectors largely because of their excellent print quality (like the Kodascope releases they were all printed on amber film stock) and their comparative rarity. Not many have survived, which suggests that they were never popular with 16mm projector owners. Generally they are less common than Kodascope films.

1941 was a black year for future collectors, for this was the year when the Kodascope Library in Britain closed its doors forever. There were several reasons for this: there was a shortage of personnel to man what was a luxury service, there were vague worries that the films represented a fire risk in air raids (ill-founded in view of the non-flam base), and one suspects Kodak saw little future in hiring outdated silent films while during wartime it was inappropriate to launch a modern sound film concept. Stacks of reels of silent features awaited cremation, the ashes used for silver recovery. To collectors it seems wantonly destructive to burn films that might prove to be irreplaceable in the future, especially as their future commercial possibilities as cinema releases were mostly nil. Probably many of the titles destroyed have disappeared forever. But there was a happy ending for some of these features: those subjects in which Kodak had the selling rights, but had not chosen to use when the library was operative, were sold to photographic dealers to use in their own libraries. The big libraries like Wallace Heaton were able to increase their scope, and the prints they did not want were offered to the public. Fortunately many of the subjects that did become available were some of the most popular Kodascope releases.

One company that made good use of the Kodascope films was a South London firm called Williams and Ivey. They not only operated a library, but also sold copies of many of the Kodascope and Ensign releases to other libraries throughout the country. Generally the quality of these dupes made by the reversal process from the amber print originals was tolerable, but when compared with the originals' sparkling quality they are a poor reflection with their grey highlights and muddy shadows. Because these dupes were so widely sold to dealer libraries, when these libraries were sold off in the Fifties and Sixties—largely as a result of television—many of the prints were sold to collectors. These 16mm copies can be identified by the fact that they are not on amber stock, they often have re-made main titles (and sometimes sub-titles) and occasionally the main titles are changed (for example Laurel and Hardy's *Do Detectives Think*? became *The Bodyguards*). The Williams and Ivey dupes are more commonly found than amber prints, though from usually bearing the same titles they can be confused with the more desirable Kodascope originals. Like other 16mm prints, they have been used as pre-print material for producing 8mm copies giving reproductions with the degraded images of the duped masters.

In addition to Williams and Ivey's re-issues there were other interesting "exclusive" titles. The British cinema was represented by Hepworth's *Tansy* (1921), another evocation of the unspoilt English countryside, and *Almost a Lady* (1928), directed by Thomas Bentley, had popular British star Mabel Poulton as a dancer who tries to mix in society. Even more collectable are Leni Reifenstahl's beautiful legend of the Dolomites, *The Blue Light* (made in 1934 but virtually a silent movie), and *The Terror* (1925), a rare feature made by Pearl White in France long after her success in serials in the States. Perhaps best of all is *The House of Arne* (1919)—Mauritz Stiller's Swedish masterpiece, a movie in advance of its time with its fluid camerawork, subtle acting style, and sense of atmosphere. Unfortunately, the copy of this film was made from a private

collector's incomplete original 35mm print, so that not only is the famous sequence of the icebound ship and the funeral of the young girl in the snow missing,
but the story's end is completely lost. Nevertheless, the strength of this film
overcomes the loss of footage, and this version, being prepared directly from an
excellent 35mm original, is well printed enough to preserve the photographic
qualities of Stiller's superb cinematographer, J. Julius.

By the early Sixties, the films from most of the 16mm silent libraries were
sold off to collectors and have either remained in private collections or have
circulated since then. The last major 16mm silent library in Britain was the
Wallace Heaton library. This was sold off in 1973 when this company merged
with a major national photographic dealer, though most of the prints available
were duplicates of the original Wallace Heaton Library copies. There were few
original Kodascope amber prints other than obscure educational subjects. And
so with this closure the last source of vintage 16mm silent prints finally dried up.

9.5mm and Pathéscope

"Le cinéma chez soi" was the slogan used when the earliest advertisements of Pathé Cinema heralded the introduction of the new 9.5mm gauge in France. And it really was the first conception of the cinema designed purely for use in the home (Pathé's 28mm was as much intended for churches, clubs, etc., as for domestic use). Christened Pathé Baby, the 9.5mm system—consisting of a projector and specially prepared films to show on it—was first seen in advertisements at the end of 1922. There was no mention of a camera; this was to follow later. Right from the start, 9.5mm was intended primarily as a home entertainer and educator rather than as an amateur movie-making medium—a fundamental principle that was exactly the opposite of Kodak's 16mm gauge, basically intended for shooting films at a moderate cost.

Charles Pathé laid great stress on his new baby, putting in charge of the operation one of his first collaborators, Ferdinand Zecca. Zecca, who was originally hired by Pathé in 1895 for his resonant voice, to be used on Pathé phonograph records of the speeches of the famous, was first employed on the movie side of the Pathé empire to explain the action on the screen in pre-subtitle days. Before long he had graduated to direction and made the early hit, *The Story of a Crime*, proving that crime on the movies paid well. In more reverent vein he was responsible for the 1908 box-office sell-out, *The Life of Christ*. Later Zecca was put in charge of the American outpost of the Pathé organisation, Pathé Exchange, returning to France in 1920 to head the Pathé Baby operation until it was well established in 1925.

Central to Pathé's 9.5mm gauge was the projector, called appropriately the Pathé Baby. It was quite unlike any of the portable projectors that had already appeared, small and compact, taking in its original form films that were only 30 ft. long. These films were permanently mounted in what we would now call a cassette, with the end of the film securely attached to the core of the container. The projector was self-threading: once the film was positioned in the gate, the operator started cranking—the machine was hand-cranked—and the film was attached to the take-up spool automatically. At the end of the reel, the operator was able to rapidly rewind a film by means of a highly geared crank in the projector head. Illumination was by means of a low voltage lamp, fed from the mains supply through a resistance. Altogether this little projector, though simple to use, was extremely well designed. Its intermittent mechanism was identical with that used by Lumière in 1896, giving remarkably steady pictures on the screen.

Top left, introducing the Pathé Baby projector
Above, the distinctive Pathé Baby 30 ft. cassette

Left, a Pathe notched title
Below, the Pathé stencil colour laboratory, Vincennes, c. 1912.

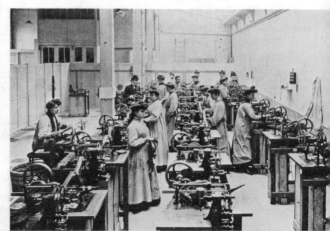

The most unusual feature of the Pathé Baby projector was its "notched title" device, already described. Although the idea worked well, it had a snag: the illumination on the screen had to be kept low as a more powerful lamp would damage the title frames. As we shall see, it was this handicap that resulted in the obsolescence of the notched title conception when home movie operators began to demand more powerful illumination for shows outside the family circle.

Performing Dogs was the first title in the Pathé Baby catalogue. Hardly a very exciting subject, it consisted merely of a few shots of trained dogs balancing on their front and hind paws. Title number two is *Miss Flutter*, a movie obviously dating back to the first decade of the century. This has a single take of a buxom young woman—apparently a music-hall performer—as a kind of human butterfly, flapping her wings which slowly change shape and colour. Colour? you may ask. And here we have another astonishing innovation in the infancy of the 9.5mm gauge.

To digress, at the turn of the century it was quite common for the short films of the time to be available in hand-coloured versions (many of the Méliès films, for example, could be obtained in this form). As the length of films increased, it soon became obvious that the labour involved, usually highly skilled girl colourists, were no longer able to cope with the demand. So the ever-inventive Pathé organisation came along with the Pathé colour system. In this method the colours were applied by stencils. A girl operator inspected each frame of the film in a magnifying viewer, cutting out with a sharp tool an area equal to the colour required for a certain detail within the frame on a special stencil film. It might require several stencil runs—each bearing a colour appropriate to various parts of the scene (flesh tints, green for foliage, blue for sky, etc.). After this preparation, an ordinary black and white print was run through a transfer machine several times, each time a separate colour being applied through the appropriate stencil. Although all this sounds crude and impractical, in fact it worked extremely well and was operated by Pathé for some of their theatrical releases right up to the time when true natural colour processes like Technicolor became a practical reality.

Stencil colour on the tiny 24mm × 18mm frames of 35mm is hard to believe, yet Pathé Baby introduced 9.5mm stencil colour for some of their earliest releases. Here again the results are far better than can be imagined and the 9.5mm stencil colour films that have survived really preserve the unique look of this fascinating process, resembling animated tinted postcards.

Unlike the truly photographic natural colour processes which are unstable, the Pathé colour tints seem to have stood the test of time without fading or bleaching. These short 30 ft. Pathé colour 9.5mm subjects are, needless to say, highly desirable collector's items. They are identifiable by the band on the 30 ft. cassettes in which they are to be found, having the title printed in silver on black. No Pathé colour films were made with English titles; those available have French titles and subjects include the aforementioned *Miss Flutter, The Le Papillon*

Machaon (the metamorphosis of a chrysalis to butterfly), *Toilettes du Soir* (a mannequin display of Paris evening fashions of 1922), *Le Lis du Japon* (a Japanese lily), *Les Anemone de Mer*) (sea anemones), *Les Gorges du Tarn*.

True to form, Pathé Baby made their first multi-reel feature on 9.5mm, *The Life of Jesus*, which appeared in thirty-two 30 ft. parts. This version of Pathé's early Passion play reveals the pioneer movie to be a quaint affair full of miracles stage-managed in a manner reminiscent of Méliès trick films. In secular vein, the first American movie to reach 9.5mm was *L'Afrique Maître Coq*, featuring Afrique (as Pathé re-named "Sunshine Sammy" Ernie Morrison, the little coloured boy featured in Hal Roach comedies in the early Twenties). Needless to say, the first major star to reach Pathé Baby was Charlie Chaplin in *Charlot et le Mari Jaloux* (with Charlie flirting on a park bench, from the 1914 Keystone *Recreation*). More Chaplin 30 ft. reels followed with extracts from *A Gentleman of Nerve, His Prehistoric Past, The Property Man*, etc. Soon the Pathé Exchange stars Harold Lloyd, Bebe Daniels and Snub Pollard joined the Pathé Baby range with Bebe in *Les Flirts de Miss Daniels* and Harold in *La Vie n'est pas toujours drôle* (from *From Hand to Mouth*, 1919). Early animated cartoons were represented by R. Lortac who used cut-out techniques for the strange surrealistic adventures of his Professor Mechanicas in several 30 ft. extracts. The delightful French comedian Marcel Levesque (remembered for brilliant work in the Feuillade serials, *The Vampires* and *Judex*) appeared in a couple of the tiny shorts as Serpentine in *Serpentine et son Modèle* and *La Rêve de Serpentine*. The first major drama to appear, and a film of considerable interest as an example of pre First World War film production shot on location in and around Paris was *L'Histoire de Jean Morande*, in sixteen 30 ft. parts. Pathé Baby also had the famous *La Mort du Duc de Guise* of 1908, the first production of Film D'Art and the first time stage actors of La Comédie Française condescended to appear on the screen. It had further claim to fame as the first movie to have a score specially composed for it by an eminent man of music, Saint Saens. Charles Pathé is said to have been so moved at this pretentious attempt at canned theatre, he told its producers with tears in his eyes, "Ah, gentlemen, you are our masters."

Considering that Max Linder was probably Pathé's greatest pre-war star, it is said to find that there were comparatively few of his comedies released in the early Pathé Baby days. The fragments that were issued included *Deux Coqs Vivaient en paix* (a couple of bachelors happily share a home until a pretty new maid arrives); *Max Linder, Amateur Photographe* (Max trying to snap his stout girl friend on the beach); *Une bonne farce* (an early version—*c*1910—of the celebrated mirror gag in which Max's manservant impersonates his reflection when a mirror is broken); and some others. All these Max Linder rarities have considerable interest for collectors.

Predominating in the 30 ft. cassette era of the Pathé Baby were the documentaries covering an incredible range of subjects from the natural history records of *The Sacred Beetle* and *The Tamandua* (a kind of South American Sloth), the

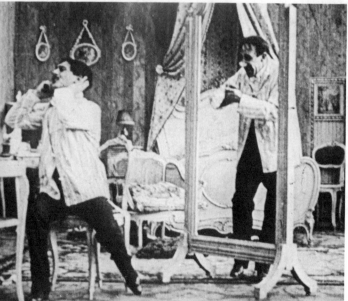

*Max Linder. Below,
the mirror gag from*
Une Bonne Farce.

newsreel items of *The Victory Celebration* (1919) and the *Carpentier–Kid Lewis Boxing Match* (1923), the industrial processes of *Tortoise Shell Comb Making* and *The Manufacture of Shaving Soap*, sport like *Duck Hunting by Aeroplane* (!), to perhaps the finest of all, the travel subjects shot well before the First World War depicting ways of life in Europe and elsewhere as part of a world yet to be dominated by the motor car, subjects like *A Trip to Alsace, Venice—Its Canals,* and many others. In fact, in this extraordinary series of subjects, primarily intended for use in schools, there's everything from *The Germination of the Broad Bean* to *Building a Ship of Ferro-Concrete.*

Not all these subjects so far mentioned were released with English titles, though it is not uncommon to find the more unusual French titled 30 ft. subjects in Britain, even today. In fact, the 30 ft. notched reels are probably the most commonly found of 9.5mm films. For some reason there are film collectors who fight shy of them, believing them to be naive and too full of titles. But they are worthy of attention, their picture quality is always good, sometimes outstanding, and despite their age—most of them were printed well over forty years ago—they are still surprisingly reasonable in price. Because the early owners of Pathé Baby projectors invariably purchased them to provide entertainment in the home, they also bought a selection of these short subjects which were cheap enough to own in quantity. The result is that when these films come up for sale, they are in sizeable batches rather than an odd reel or so. A fortunate collector may be lucky enough to find a projector together with, say, thirty or forty of these fascinating little cassettes.

In 1924, the Pathé Baby projector and films were introduced in Britain by Pathé of France, later called Pathéscope Ltd. At about this time, the maximum length that the Pathé projector could handle was increased to 60 feet, and films began to be released in 60 ft. cassettes as well as the original 30 ft. format. The longer basic reel unit made it possible to prepare fuller versions of films, with the result that in this second phase of the 9.5mm story there was increased scope in the range of subjects available.

Before proceeding with the details of what was to become one of the most interesting periods of 9.5mm, it is appropriate to look at one of the most controversial aspects of 9.5mm releases—the question of cutting. One of the distinctive features of Pathé 9.5mm films was that they were nearly all cut versions of the originals. The reason for cutting was that, unlike the various distributors of 16mm who only made their films available for hire, Pathé's policy was to make all their releases for sale to collectors, and shortening the originals enabled them to sell versions priced with the reach of Pathé Baby projector owners. Present day collectors, exasperated at the whims of Pathé's editors, should pause to reflect that only the reasonable price of 9.5mm cut versions ensured they were sold in large enough numbers to make them still available. Comparing the 9.5mm prints still to be found with the rarer vintage 16mm movies underlines the wisdom of Pathé's policy.

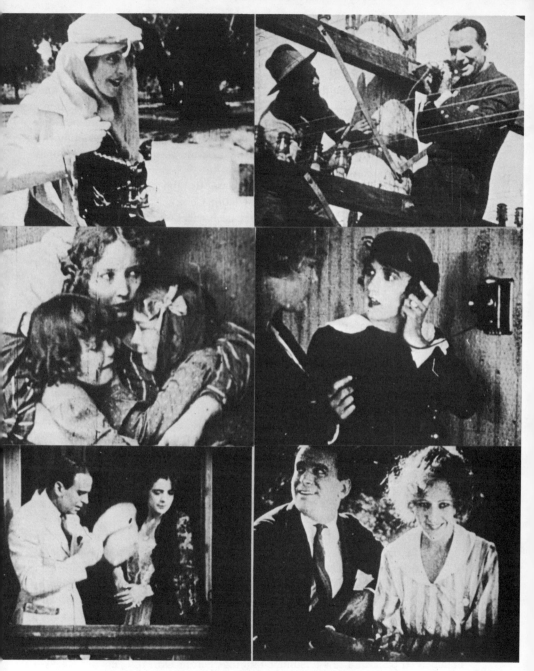

Frames from Triangle movies. Top left, Enid Bennett in They're Off.
Top right, Douglas Fairbanks in The Matrimaniac.
Middle left, Bessie Love in A Sister of Six.
Middle right, Constance Talmadge in The Matrimaniac.
Bottom left, Douglas Fairbanks and Alma Rubens in The Americano.
Bottom right, Douglas Fairbanks and Jewel Carmen in American Aristocracy.

In many of the Pathé condensations, the major loss is the sub-plots rather than the real meat of the film. The editing is most damaging to the tempo and montage of the original, and moving camera work often suffers at the cutter's hands. But because of their excellent print quality, the abridged 9.5mm versions are extremely kind to the original photography, a fact probably explaining the popularity of 9.5mm prints among British collectors who are also professional cameramen.

By 1926, 9.5mm was well established in Britain, with Pathéscope Ltd. prospering under the leadership of Jean-Claude Cabirol, its enthusiastic French managing director. There was a comprehensive selection of films available with English titles, batches of new subjects being issued every month. Many were in the new 60 ft. format, particularly interesting being a series of multi-reel 60 ft. versions of American Triangle productions. The Triangle Corporation, which survived from 1915 to 1917, gathered together the three leading film-makers of the day, D. W. Griffith, Mack Sennett, and Thomas H. Ince, as well as a host of famous stage actors and some up and coming movie players to produce an ambitious output of films on a scale new to Hollywood. Although considerably abbreviated, the Triangle subjects on 9.5mm were cleverly edited to leave something of the flavour of the originals. The Douglas Fairbanks subjects were particularly effective in this respect, with a generous portion of Doug's famous acrobatic stunts left intact. *The Matrimaniac* (9.5mm title: *A Telephone Marriage*) has him using telephone wires as a tightrope so that he can get to the phone to marry Constance Talmadge by proxy; *The Americano* (1916, 9.5mm title: *The American*) features a splendid fist fight with Doug diving from a table to deal with the henchmen of a tyrannical Latin American dictator.

In more romantic vein there was Norma Talmadge impersonating a lady's maid in *A Social Secretary* (9.5mm title: *A Lady's Companion*), with Erich von Stroheim in a supporting role as a sneaky journalist. *Station Content* (9.5mm title: *The Tempest*), with one of Gloria Swanson's earliest dramatic roles, is a soap opera. For its climax, Gloria bravely flags down "The Limited" to stop it crashing after a bridge has been damaged by lightning. The charming *They're Off* (9.5mm title: *Milady The Jockey*) has pretty Enid Bennett masquerading as a jockey to turn the tables on her father after he has ruined a plantation owner by his Wall Street dealings. In *Little Meena's Romance* (9.5mm title: *Minnie's Romance*), there is Dorothy Gish as a Pennsylvanian Dutch girl who falls for a washing salesman—played by Owen Moore—and then later discovers she's become an heiress. In the space of 120 feet of film, this pleasant light comedy manages to pack in a few misunderstandings before Dorothy gets her legacy—and wins her man.

There were other Pathéscope Triangle releases featuring Charles Ray, Bessie Love, Frank Keenan and Wallace Reid, and there were several westerns starring William S. Hart from the Thomas H. Ince apex. Because 9.5mm was very reliant on movies from the Continent, these short versions of this interesting phase in Hollywood's history are among the most important American films to be issued on the gauge.

Not so successful was Pathéscope's attempt at converting Flaherty's master-piece *Nanook Of The North* into a conventional notched title "educational" film under the title of *Esquimaux*. Most of the rhythm and charm of Flaherty's greatest documentary is lost in the choppy editing, though occasionally sequences like the building of the igloo manage to survive reasonably intact.

The 60 ft. format was the source of many outstanding releases in France, most of which were not released with English titles. There were several of Abel Gance's early films like *Le Droit à la Vie* (1917), *Mater Dolorosa* (1917), *La Dixième Symphonie* (1918), and *J'Accuse* (1918), his superb anti-war movie. Even though they were strictly covered by copyright—at least in Britain and America—there was Chaplin's *The Pilgrim* (1922), and also *Pay Day* (1921) from Chaplin's First National period. From Warner Brothers came the Darryl F. Zanuck-scripted *The Lighthouse by the Sea* (9.5mm title: *Rin Tin Tin Gardien du Phare*) featuring the four-footed star that kept Warners' from bankruptcy, the highly popular Rin Tin Tin. The only existing version of George Pearson's *Satan's Sister* (9.5mm title: *Bohemiens de la Mère*) (1925), with Betty Balfour— inexplicably never released in Britain—has been discovered in France by a British collector (and a 16mm master has been made from it for preservation purposes), one of many instances where the 9.5mm version is the only one now available.

In 1928, the demand for movies that gave more satisfying entertainment than the scrappy 30 ft. and 60 ft. presentations encouraged the development of an attachment for the Pathé Baby projector, making it possible for it to take reels equivalent in length to a thousand feet of 35mm—a standard reel, in fact. Known as a Super Attachment, this well designed device accommodated these long reels, avoiding all the continual re-winding that was the weakness of the cassette system. The introduction of longer reels increased the scope of 9.5mm as a collectors' gauge, bringing it more into line with 16mm. It is these movies released on 300 ft. reels from 1928 onwards that are in most demand by collec-tors. Called Super Reels by Pathéscope, these reels are identified by catalogue numbers prefixed by S/. Thus S/600 is a Super Reel with notched titles.

Between 1928 and 1934, most of the greatest films to reach 9.5mm were released by Pathéscope. Everything seemed to be working well for the gauge at this time; the choice of subjects was excellent and the skill of the Pathéscope laboratory resulted in prints of outstanding quality even though the new, longer versions were still abridgements of the original films. Initially most of the Super Reel versions were in one or two reels only, and like the shorter films already issued had the standardised Pathé titles (a form of presentation that was inevi-table in view of the many foreign language versions released by Pathé throughout the world).

French movies predominated in the first of the batches of Super Reel

Above, frames from Baroncelli's Pêcheurs d'Islande.
Below, Pathe's standardised title styles.

PATHESCOPE
presents
CAPTAIN BLOOD.
Drama in Two Parts.
(Super Reels.)

"BABY CINE"
presents
KŒNIGSMARK
A Super Reel Drama
in Two Parts.
Adapted from the Novel by
Pierre BENOIT.

Raquel Meller in
The Oppressed.

releases, the very first being number S/525 *To Be or Not To Be* (1922), a naval drama chiefly distinguished by a sequence of the mining of a submarine (obligingly issued as *The Loss of a Submarine* in a 30 ft. cassette for those projector owners without a Super Attachment). One of the most beautiful of these early silent features was *Pêcheurs d'Islande* (1923—9.5mm title: *The Fishers of the Isle*) directed by Jacques de Baroncelli from Pierre Loti's famous novel. With its carefully composed photography of the Breton coast and affectionately observed details of the customs of Brittany, it builds up a strong sense of the effects of the rugged landscape and stormy seas on the lives of the fishing community. Sandra Milowanoff and veteran Charles Vanel play the tragic lovers in this minor classic.

Abel Gance's extraordinary tragedy *La Roue* (1922—9.5mm title: *The Wheel*) with its unfortunate engine driver, who saves a little girl from a railway wreck and when she grows up into a beautiful woman falls madly in love with her, had its dramatic highlights concentrated into two reels. Gance's famed rapid cutting is missing in this short version, but in the longer four reel edition only issued in France, there is at least a chance to see more of cinematographer Burel's impressively photographed railway and mountain scenes. Although not in the same league as Gance, the 9.5mm versions of the films of Henri Roussel have some merit for collectors. A commercial director of erratic talent, Roussel made his name with *Violettes Imperiales* (1924), an operetta-like story of a little flower seller saving the Empress Eugenie from an anarchist's bomb. It starred Raquel Meller, the Spanish music hall singer who was the rage of Paris in the early Twenties, and she appeared again for Roussel in *The Oppressed* (1924), concerning the plight of the Flemish under Spanish rule in the 16th Century; she is the Spanish governor's daughter in love with a Flemish resistance leader. Once again it is not unlike an opera with its flamboyant gestures and elaborate costumes. *The Promised Land* (1925) deals with the problems of racial prejudice in

its story of a Polish-Jewish oil-well owner in conflict with his workers, again
starring Raquel Meller, this time with her sister Tina. Directed with a true feeling
for the cinema with its skilled playing and fluid camerawork, it is totally different
in style to Roussel's silent "operas". It was unusual, too, for the French cinema
of the time to concern itself with controversial and thought-provoking themes.
Roussel continued this promising trend with *L'Ile Enchantée* (1927—9.5mm title:
Vendetta) where the building of a hydroelectric scheme threatens the unspoilt
environment of some Corsican farmers. But Roussel's version of an episode in
Napoleon's career, *Destiny* (1925), was a disaster. Quite the opposite was Abel
Gance's *Napoleon vu par Abel Gance* (1927), released by Pathéscope in four complete episodes, under the titles *Napoleon Bonaparte's Youth* (one reel), *Napoleon
Bonaparte and the French Revolution* (two reels), *Napoleon—The Road to Glory*
(two reels), and *Napoleon—The Siege of Toulon* (one reel). Although these six
reels represent a portion of the original, the Pathéscope version is intelligently
edited and by no means an unworthy souvenir of this momentous French silent
movie. *The French Revolution* is the best of the episodes, retaining the incredible
Marseillaise sequence, the daring cutting between Napoleon in a storm at sea and
the stormy meeting of the Convention, and the assassination of Marat, with
Antonin Artaud as the diseased revolutionary murdered in his bath. Albert

Director Abel Gance as St. Just in Napoléon.

The assassination of Marat from Napoléon (Marguerite Gance, the director's wife, as Charlotte Corday).

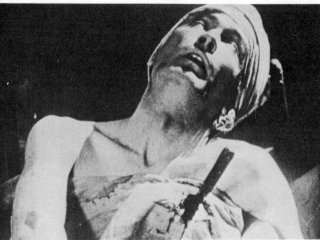

Above, frames from La Marseillaise sequence in Napoléon.
Below, the macabre climax to The Chess Player.

Dieudonné plays Napoleon superbly in Gance's epic film, though originally it was intended that Ivan Mosjoukine should be given the part. It was probably a wise decision not to have the Russian actor in the role as his distinctive acting style would have swamped the part. A number of Mosjoukine's unusual films are on 9.5mm. However, they are discussed in detail in Part 4.

Raymond Bernard's excellent historic drama, *The Chess Player* (1927), part fact, part fantasy, made an outstanding two reel release. Although drastically cut, it retains in full the horrific climax of the villain trapped in the strange hall of the mysterious Baron Kempelen, encircled by life size automata—dressed as soldiers—who slash him to death with their cutlasses. In France, this fascinating movie was issued in three reels, a rarity keenly sought by British collectors. The talented Belgian director Jacques Feyder was represented by *Gribiche* (1925), a pleasant comedy drama with a clever child actor, Jean Forest, supporting Françoise Rosay (the director's wife). Feyder's *Visages d'Enfants* (1923—9.5mm title: *Mists of Error*), a moving story of a boy—Jean Forest again—brought up by a spiteful stepmother, was attractively shot on location in Switzerland, and one of the first movies to extract a strong dramatic performance from a child. Feyder's *Carmen* (1927), superbly photographed on location in Spain, failed to be totally effective because Raquel Meller quarrelled with the director on her interpretation of the classic role. Not only did she play the *femme fatale* too sympathetically, but she failed to radiate any sex appeal on the screen. But a fight with daggers and the duel between Don José and the Lieutenant are handled with mastery and there is no hint of the opera here—they are true cinema. A four reel version of *Carmen* only issued in France provides a far better insight into the characters than the two reel English release.

René Clair—one of France's greatest directors—was represented by three of his silent movies. *Le Voyage Imaginaire* (1924—9.5mm title: *Such Stuff as Dreams Are Made Of*) is pure fantasy. A timid bank clerk dreams he is in Fairyland where his office rivals are trouble-makers, and the reluctant kisses he gives to a row of old crones transforms them into a line-up of glamorous show girls. Cut to one reel, this amusing comedy preserves inventive detail like an old lady customer's eccentric car (straight from the magic world of Méliès), and the exotic underground Fairyland settings. Turning aside from comedy in his experimental period, Clair freshened up the routine melodramatics of *La Proie du Vent* (1925—9.5mm title: *The Mystery of the Lone Castle*). A dream sequence of Charles Vanel imagining the events behind the locked doors of the chateau, where he is recuperating after an aeroplane crash, has the action shot against stylised gauze draperies. There is also a stunning car chase culminating in a rapidly cut montage with shots as brief as a single frame. Only two reels are available—and one constantly wishes for more—but this short version is probably all there is of this movie likely to be seen today; the complete film has not been revived since the Twenties.

Best known of René Clair's silent films is *The Italian Straw Hat* (1927—

Above, *a modernistic fairyland in Clair's* Le Voyage Imaginaire
Below, frames from the rare La Proie du Vent *with Sandra Milowanoff and Charles Vanel*

9.5mm title: *The Leghorn Hat*). On the way to his wedding, Albert Préjean's horse eats a lady's straw hat while she is in the Bois de Boulogne with her soldier lover. Threatened with dire consequences by the soldier, the harassed bridegroom has to replace the hat before the lady's husband finds out. With such delightful characters as the jovial deaf uncle, the cuckold wearing the wrong boots, and the henpecked husband with the slipping neck-tie, this comedy based on the stage farce by Labiche and Michel spins along with all the pace of a Sennett two-reeler. The two reel Pathéscope version was one of their most successful abridgements, its interest increased by the clever cartoons used to illustrate all the subtitles.

Also revived on 9.5mm are the totally overlooked comedies of Nicholas Rimsky, a compatriot of Mosjoukine who came to France with the émigrés from Russia. Balding, middle-aged Rimsky, with h's slightly puzzled manner, turned out several enjoyable comedies in the mid-Twenties with a flavour all of their own. In *Le Heureuse Mort* (9.5mm title: *Dead and Alive*), he is an unsuccessful playwright falling out of a friend's launch at sea. Accepted as drowned, his reputation soars— and the town hall raises a statue for him—but really he is alive and well, enjoying a country existence. Gently mocking art snobs and local government bigwigs, this movie reminds one of British comedies from Ealing Studios two decades later. *The Porter at Maxim's* has him as the doorman at the famous Parisian restaurant. On the strength of his tips, he leads a double life as the owner of a large country chateau. A bright reminder of the high-life in the Twenties this likeable comedy is Rimsky's best. American tourists come in for some mild satire in *Paris in Five Days*. One of its smartest gags has the tourists arriving at the Louvre to hurtle through on a whistle-stop tour, all shot at eight frames per second!

A weakness of the Pathéscope range of movies was the lack of first-class American subjects. There was nothing at all from the major production companies like Paramount and Fox; those American titles that did appear tended to come from Poverty Row outfits like Gotham and Preferred Pictures. Despite their humble origins, some of these B movies do have points of interest for collectors. For example, Preferred Pictures' *Exclusive Rights* (1926—9.5mm title: *The Bickel Affair*) handles an anti-capital punishment theme against a background of a sleazy night club, complete with chubby chorus girls and real-life burlesque comic Jimmy Savo. Gayne Whitman—an accomplished player who seemed doomed to a career in Gower Gulch (as late as 1941 he was still in featured roles for PRC)—is the prison governor sending his best friend to the electric chair to force a confession from a gangster. Some action in the prison death row makes this a precursor of the kind of movie cranked out by Warner Brothers a decade later. Another Preferred production, *Dancing Days* (1926), is a neat little soap opera with Lillian Rich as a dance-crazy blonde leading a stuffy husband astray; it took a critical look at the Charleston set.

Gotham's movies handled less interesting ideas, concentrating on rather

"That's a very badly brought up family of yours!"

Scenes from The Italian Straw Hat. *Top left, horse eats hat — Albert Préjean.*
Top right, compromised lady (Olga Tschechova) and soldier lover.
Left, the gag with the slipping necktie.
Right, the unique titles that are a feature of the 9.5mm versions of Clair's *silent masterpiece.*

Left, Nicholas Rimsky, The Porter at Maxim's.
Right, gangsters 1926 style — Exclusive Rights.

corny melodrama. But somehow their productions revive the spirit of the days when movies were uncomplicated fun and thrills, like *Overland Ltd.* (1926—9.5mm title: *The Mad Train*) with its cliff-hanging finale triggered off by a jealous architect weakening the structure of a bridge built by his engineer rival. It turns out that his aged mother is on board a train speeding towards the dangerous bridge, and—the ultimate twist—an escaped lunatic has over-powered the driver and taken over the controls . . . This naive film moves at a cracking pace with a classic piece of Griffith cutting leading to a last-minute averting of disaster. Another Gotham melodrama, *The Silent Avenger* (1927—9.5mm title: *Good Dog*), featured a dog advertised by Pathéscope in an out-rageous piece of misrepresentation as Rin Tin Tin. Actually this hound, Gotham's "Thunder," is by no means a bad performer—almost the equal of Warners' four footed talent; only the production values of the big studio are missing in this cut-price actioner.

There is one particular batch of long-forgotten American subjects unique to the gauge, movies from the autumn years of what had been one of the greatest of the pre-First World War producers—Vitagraph, founded in 1896 by two Englishmen, J. Stuart Blackton and Albert E. Smith. By the early Twenties this long-established company was fighting for survival in competition with newer, more aggressive producers. In many ways their films were old-fashioned compared with the more sophisticated output of the new studios, but they were well made, solid productions with excellent photography and settings. Most spectacular of the Pathéscope Vitagraphs was *Captain Blood* (1924), with pioneer movie actor J. Warren Kerrigan in the title role. Lacking the sheer entertain-ment of Michael Curtiz' version of eleven years later (and Kerrigan is no Errol Flynn), it can boast some fine sea battles with full scale galleons. It was directed by David Smith who had some of Vitagraph's best assignments. He also made *Black Beauty* (1921—9.5mm title: *Black Bess*), a convincing version of the children's classic; and an interesting old-time melodrama climaxed by a locomotive thundering through a forest fire, *The Ninety and Nine* (1922—9.5mm title: *Through Fire*), the only chance to see Warner Baxter and Colleen Moore together. This is a particularly rare item, for some reason never officially issued in Britain.

In the final stages of Vitagraph before it was taken over by Warner Brothers, founder member J. Stuart Blackton took to direction again and turned in three major movies. *Tides of Passion* (1925—9.5mm title: *The Sea Repays*) demonstrates Vitagraph's flair for impressive special effects with a violent gale against which Mae Marsh struggles to rescue her feckless husband's mistress from drowning. Based on a best seller of the Twenties, *The Happy Warrior* (1925—9.5mm title: *The Heir*), is an involved tale about a disputed legacy, particularly effective in its scenes of a fire at a circus. The most memorable of the Blackton trio is *The Beloved Brute* (1925—9.5mm title: *Unto the Strong*) with Victor McLaglen making his American debut. Reminiscent of Fellini's *La Strada*, it had

The Ninety and Nine *with
Colleen Moore and Warner
Baxter*.

The Beloved Brute with Victor
McLaglen.

Vitagraph's version of **The**
Magnificent Ambersons,
called Pampered Youth. *Here
the serenade scene, closely
copied in Welles' version of
Booth Tarkington's novel.*

McLaglen as a wrestler, the companion of a girl dancer and a gypsy fortune teller, travelling from town to town in a caravan and giving shows. But probably the most fascinating of all the Vitagraph movies today is *Pampered Youth* (1925—9.5mm title: *Two to One*), David Smith's version of Booth Tarkington's "The Magnificent Ambersons." Its earlier scenes are sometimes close to those in Welles's masterpiece and later there is an astonishingly realistic fire (not in Welles's version), quite brilliantly directed.

Pathéscope treated these Vitagraph movies in a curious way, possibly because there was some doubt as to the ownership of their rights, altering their main titles and even the names of characters in the stories. Only the painstaking work of film collectors and researchers has revealed the true origins of these well disguised movies for the benefit of fellow enthusiasts. Pathéscope's coverage of American comedy shorts was equally eccentric. There were the inevitable Chaplin shorts, but the choice of other comedies was haphazard. Harold Lloyd was given reasonable treatment with a selection of his early Hal Roach produced shorts, including *Over the Fence* (1917), the very first movie in which he wore his famous trademark, the horn-rimmed glasses. Harold and his partner Snub Pollard are a couple of tailors finding tickets to a baseball game in a customer's pocket, with the third member of the team, Bebe Daniels, as Harold's doting girl friend at the match. Bebe has one of her best moments in *For Daisy's Bright Eyes* (true title unknown): as a sultry flirt with a group of middle-aged wolves tailing her, she makes for the park, reaches a lake, then neatly sidesteps so that her eager admirers all fall in for a soaking. American comedy owes a debt to the model T Ford. Long suffering tin lizzies were bent, battered, and generally humiliated, all in the cause of laughs. In *Get Out and Get Under* (1921—9.5mm title: *My Very Own Car*), Harold is the absurdly proud owner of a sparkling model T. Sly digs at the cult of car worship lead to hilarious action when the car runs out of control down a steep hill with Harold in hot pursuit.

Take hair-raising action, play it for laughs, and you have the formula for the "thrill" comedy—Harold Lloyd's most famous gimmick. In *Never Weaken*

Over the Fence. *Harold Lloyd and Bebe Daniels.*

(1921—9.5mm title: *A Trip to Paradise*), Harold, thinking he has been jilted, "shoots" himself and is whisked out of his office on a swinging girder to the top of a partly built skyscraper. With acrobatic skill, he goes through nerve-wracking gags as he misses his hold on girders, ladders, and ropes. A set built over a tunnel mouth and a careful choice of camera angle, intercut with vertical shots of the streets below, gives a dizzy illusion of height without recourse to process photography. His first feature, *Grandma's Boy* (1922—9.5mm title: *Le Talisman de Grandmaman*—only issued in France), is unusually restrained, almost a comedy drama, and comparable with Keaton's *The General*. Cowardly Harold learns bravery with the aid of a good luck charm, actually the knob off his grandma's umbrella! Realistically constructed small town settings and a flashback to the Civil War make this one of Lloyd's most novel films.

Charley Chase, another Hal Roach comic, appeared in a number of titles but Pathéscope would insist on calling Chase Paul Parrott, and at the same time issuing comedies by the real Paul Parrott. Actually they could be partly forgiven for this confusion: both Charley Chase and Paul Parrott were Hal Roach comedians, and they were brothers with a certain facial resemblance. To add to the muddle, Paul Parrott was really James Parrott, who abandoned his career as a comic to become a director (later handling many of Laurel and Hardy's best sound shorts). Some of the true Paul Parrott comedies are quite good, particularly *Shiver and Shake*—a typical Roach "spook" comedy—and *Do Your Stuff* with its high jinks in Chinatown. Pathéscope released Charley Chase subjects that were hardly representative of the work of this tantalising comedian who could at times be inventive and extremely funny—the equal of the great silent comics, as can be seen in some of the Robert Youngson compilations—and, at other times, be puerile. Among the Chase shorts was *Powder and Smoke* (1924—9.5mm: title *Your Money or Your Life*): Charley is a salesman of lightning rods out West, getting tangled up with some bandits and the ranch owner they are out to rob. The result is a weird comedy indeed with action developing in surrealist situations that would not look out of place in a Luis Buñuel movie. *Fraidy Cat* (1925—9.5mm title: *Paul Becomes a Caveman*) has Charley as a nervous suitor who is a coward until he thinks he only has a few days to live, a variation on the situation in *Grandma's Boy*.

Stan Laurel appeared in a few of the movies he made solo for Hal Roach before teaming with Oliver Hardy. The best is *Smithy* (9.5mm title: *Old Soldiers Never Die*) where the incompetent Stan successfully demolishes a building site. Generally, Laurel's individual appearances with his screen *persona* of brashness and stupidity are unlikeable, not to be compared with his brilliant teamwork with Hardy. Another Roach comic not to be seen other than on 9.5mm was Glenn Tryon. He rents a model T to take his girl for a spin in *The Wages of Tin* (9.5mm title: *Billy the Ford Buster*), but it disintegrates along the road. And he arrives at a haunted mansion of the "Cat and the Canary" type in *A Haunted Honeymoon* (9.5mm title: *Billy Gets Married*) for a flow of "spook" gags of a

Paul Parrott.

kind that were to provide plenty of footage over the years. Roach's Our Gang appeared in *Sundown Ltd.* (9.5mm title: *Full Steam Ahead*) and *Firefighters* (9.5mm title: *Jackie's Fire Brigade*) with locomotives and fire engines built from scrap. The nadir of the Roach output on 9.5mm was the *Dippy Do Dads*, an objectionable series featuring animals dressed up as humans.

After their excellent selection of French classics released between 1928 and 1931, Pathéscope achieved an even greater scoop in 1931, gaining the rights to the cream of the movies from the German UFA studios. This was a remarkable act of faith on their part because these movies were hardly popular fare and to issue them was far from being commercially minded. But by making these classics, many of which had only been seen by the privileged members of the Film Society, available to collectors at a moderate cost, Pathéscope were pioneering the activities of the National Film Archive (see Part Four).

It was during the UFA releasing programme that Pathéscope bowed to

As high as an elephant's eye —
Stan Laurel solo in
Roughest Africa.

Our Gang.
At top, Allen Hoskins
("Farina"). Second row:
Mickey Daniels, Johnny
Downs, Jackie Condon.
Third row: Joe Cobb,
Mary Kornman,
unidentified.

the inevitable and introduced in 1933 a powerful projector—the 200B—comparable with the competing 16mm machines. The effect on future releases was to make it no longer possible to use notched titles as the higher powered lamp would have burned the still frames. From February 1933, all the Super Reel releases were issued with conventional "running" titles. The new films had their numbers prefixed by the code SB/ (for Super Bobine), and each reel had a shorter running time than its notched equivalent; a notched Super Reel averaged about fifteen minutes, an SB reel only twelve minutes. For a while, sets of running titles were issued for splicing in place of the notched captions in some of the more popular subjects. At this time another batch of classic silent movies began to appear: the important productions made by British International Pictures around 1928 to 1930 (see Part 4).

From 1934 onwards, there was a decline in the number of truly collectable silent releases. After the highlights of the UFA and BIP programmes, collectors had to be contented with tepid British silents like *The Further Adventures of the*

Flag Lieutenant (1927), and tedious mute versions of low grade French sound movies of the early Thirties. Only *In the Name of the Law* (1933), directed by the prolific Maurice Tourneur, with the dependable Charles Vanel on the trail of drug runners, and the moving, humane *La Maternelle* (1935), by Jean Benoit Levy were worthy of Pathéscope. Very occasionally a worthwhile silent subject did appear like Jean Renoir's *Le Tournée de la Cité* (1929) proving that in the hands of a master there was plenty of life in the costume film so beloved by French directors in the Twenties. American silent comedies were reduced to the products from the bargain basement CBC, *The Hall Room Boys*, a tired series repeating gags better done by others. To meet the shortage of good live action comedy, Pathéscope negotiated for a batch of early black-and-white cartoons from Walt Disney. Ironically, these cartoons really needed sound for their full enjoyment, but they were never issued with soundtracks after the introduction of 9.5mm talkies (a Disney policy that extends to today; present day Super 8 prints of Disney shorts are only available in mute form). The Pathéscope Disney releases included Ub Iwerks's animated Mickey Mouse and Silly Symphony subjects like *The Skeleton Dance*, *The Opry House*, and *The Plough Boy*.

By the mid-Thirties, the effects of the talkie revolution were shaking the home cinema scene. The result was the introduction of 9.5mm sound, based on a well-designed projector, the Vox. Immediately on its launching in April 1938, sound subjects appeared at the unprecedented rate of twenty-five reels a month, and they could all be purchased outright. The reel unit of 300 ft. was used, giving a running time of eight minutes at sound speed. In view of the generally longer length of sound movies, many of these titles were supplied on 900 ft. reels. Catalogue numbers were prefixed T/. Among the early sound subjects, the most important are the range of *Popeye* and *Betty Boop* cartoons produced by Max Fleischer in the period 1933–1935. Unlike the Disney organisation. Fleischer and his distributor Paramount had no objection to these productions being issued with soundtracks. The *Betty Boops* are particularly attractive, backed by famous bands of the Thirties, like *The Old Man of the Mountains* with Cab Calloway and *Morning Noon and Night* with Rubinoff and his Orchestra. *I Heard* had Don Redman and his music along with Betty Boop sorting out a coal-mining problem by chasing away the "Gas Ghosts." The first major feature to appear was *Midshipman Easy*, and with this film the trend of future Pathéscope versions of sound movies was set. Like the silent subjects, they were nearly all abridgements.

Death at Broadcasting House (1934) is a murder mystery. During a broadcast, an unpleasant actor (Donald Wolfit), who is supposedly strangled in a radio play, is actually murdered. Using a magnetic recording of his performance, a Scotland Yard inspector (Ian Hunter) reconstructs the crime and nails the killer. In its original version, various popular radio artistes of the day made guest appearances, and some of these are retained in the cut 9.5mm release giving a fascinating glimpse of the BBC in action in the Thirties. Along with

HUGHIE GREEN in "MIDSHIPMAN EASY"

PATHÉSCOPE
MONTHLY
AUGUST - SEPTEMBER 1938
THE REVIEW FOR THE AMATEUR CINEMATOGRAPHER

GEORGE FORMBY in "NO LIMIT"

PATHÉSCOPE
MONTHLY
DECEMBER 1938
THE REVIEW FOR THE AMATEUR CINEMATOGRAPHER

HARRY BAUR in "MOSCOW NIGHTS"

PATHÉSCOPE
MONTHLY
APRIL - MAY 1939
THE REVIEW FOR THE AMATEUR CINEMATOGRAPHER

BELLE CHRYSTALL
and
NIALL MacGINNIS
in
"THE EDGE OF
THE WORLD"

PATHÉSCOPE
MONTHLY

9.5mm sound releases. Copies of the Pathéscope Monthly giving details of these releases are now as much sought after as the film themselves.

the feature releases, there were numerous Pathétone one reel "variety" films with stage acts which now appear nostalgic—or camp—according to your age!

Hollywood's first talkies proved there was nothing like a musical to capture an audience. So Pathéscope's response was several cheaply produced musicals featuring famous British dance bands. Negligible as films, these productions are as ephemeral as today's TV shows, and would probably be ignored had it not been that they fall into line with the cult of the "big band sound." They included *Calling All Stars* (1937) with Ambrose and Carroll Gibbons and their orchestras; *She Shall Have Music* (1935) starring the band of veteran Jack Hylton; and *Soft Lights and Sweet Music* (1936), Ambrose again with a roster of variety acts. Ahead of these dance band movies came one from an entirely different source: the British Commercial Gas Association! Advertising the Ascot gas water heater, *Happy in the Morning* (1938) stars Henry Hall and his band playing in a BBC studio while listeners throughout Britain tune in for a regular date for his music. With its numerous shots in actual homes of the Thirties, this captivating movie is not only musically enjoyable, it is a social document! Appropriately, it was produced by Alberto Cavalcanti, bringing his flair for documentary to this splendid little film.

Most popular of all the musicals on 9.5mm is *Land without Music* (1936), which one suspects is more due to its excellent soundtrack doing justice to Richard Tauber's fine tenor voice singing the Oscar Strauss music than to its merits as a film. Directed by comedy specialist Walter Forde and starring Jimmy Durante in a major role, it lacks the vital spark to make it truly memorable.

These musical programmers throw into relief three genuine classics of the British cinema of the Thirties that have been preserved on 9.5mm. *Moscow Nights* (1936), directed by Anthony Asquith, although dismissed by contemporary critics now appears as a polished production with fine performances by Laurence Olivier as a young Russian officer compromised as a spy when he gets caught with a gambling debt, and Harry Baur as the elderly *fiancé* of the girl he has fallen in love with. Michael Powell's beautifully photographed—by Ernest Palmer—*The Edge of the World* (1936) has much of the British penchant for documentary. Based on an actual incident of a Shetland island that had to be evacuated because of poor living conditions and unemployment, it has its action focussed on the conflict between the young, keen to settle on the mainland, and the old, steadfastly against migration. At the film's symbolic end, one of the elders (John Laurie) goes in search of a guillemot's egg while the boat waits to take the evacuees away from their island home, and falls to his death. The third Pathéscope talkie classic is a comedy: *No Limit* (1936) with George Formby, the beloved music hall comic with the toothy grin and cheeky songs accompanied on his banjo-ukelele. George is mad on motor bikes (actually a real-life craze of the North Country comedian), building a machine for entry in the Isle of Man Tourist Test Race. For the most part hilarious, with hair-raising motor cycle racing, it has Formby at his peak with the comedy construction firmly handled by ex-silent screen comedian Monty Banks, forging a new career as a director in Britain.

The Second World War was the start of the major down-turn in the fortunes of 9.5mm. During the war a few new subjects, mostly newsreels, came out—but for the most part it was marking time. After the war, reasonably entertaining British wartime films like *Candlelight in Algeria* (1944) and *Tomorrow We Live* (1942) appeared, and the musical drama *The Glass Mountain* (1948), set in the Dolomites, with a romantic score by Nino Rota and starring the husband and wife team of Michael Denison and Dulcie Gray, has become a collectors' classic. A throwback to the type of movie being issued before the war was *The Girl in the Poster*; extracted from the obscure British musical of 1938, *Rhythm Racketeers*, it has Harry Roy, the dance band leader in a production number that cleverly duplicates the Busby Berkeley style. Crafty camera angles—with many overhead shots—and lively cutting put the routine over with all the panache of Berkeley.

Another innovation was the release of American features, films like *Emergency Landing* (1941), an aeroplane actioner with Forrest Tucker, and Bela Lugosi cheapies, *Ghosts in the Night* (1943) and *The Devil Bat* (1940), from Monogram and PRC. Later, a few of the Sol Wurtzel B pictures originally released by Twentieth Century-Fox appeared, notably *Dangerous Years* (1948) with Marilyn Monroe at the start of her career. More unusual were *The New Adventures of Tarzan* and *Tarzan and the Green Goddess*, both cut from the 1935 serial *The New Adventures of Tarzan*. Shot on location in Guatemala, these offbeat subjects make up in authenticity what they lack in the production gloss of MGM and RKO. *Tom Brown's Schooldays* (1939) had the odd casting of Jimmy "Henry Aldrich" Lydon as Tom, and Dead End kid leader Billy Halop as Flashman, the Rugby bully. Charles Laughton had a strong supporting cast but weak direction in *Captain Kidd* (1945), and Norman Z. McLeod's version of *Little Men* (1941) with the veterans Jack Oakie, George Bancroft, and Kay Francis was yet another 9.5mm film of a book.

Hal Roach sound movies appeared in the Fifties with Laurel and Hardy's delightful features *Swiss Miss* (1936) and the underrated—but lavishly produced— *Our Relations* (1936). There was a good cross-section of five of their shorts including *Brats* (1931), notably for the clever special effects used to make the idea of Stan and Ollie appearing as a couple of boys convincing; five from Charley Chase; and five of the lower grade Taxi Boys, little more than re-runs of Roach *clichés*. The enjoyable Hal Roach feature *Kelly the Second* (1935) builts its gags around a dumb boxer, Guinn Williams, sponsored by splendidly loud-mouthed Patsy Kelly, and Charley Chase looking grey and elderly. Lower down the scale of comedy were one or two Educational Pictures (inaccurately sloganned "the Spice of the Program") made by Buster Keaton, light years away from his silent masterpieces, with only occasional reminders of the once great master of comedy.

Pathéscope's real effort was going into the sound programme, silent issues consisting of mute sub-titled Laurel and Hardy shorts, and a sprinkling of B Westerns with such minor characters as Renfrew (of the Royal Mounted) and Rin Tin Tin Junior. There was a brief attempt at reviving the success story of the past; Pathéscope managed to get hold of a few re-issue prints made on the Continent of the First National comedies of Chaplin. Unfortunately the master material had been tampered with, poor editing spoiling key scenes in these classics. *Shoulder Arms* (1918) had the major loss of the framing story (in the original it was made clear that the action at the Front was a dream), and the brilliant sequence of Charlie camouflaged as a tree on an "intelligence" mission. *The Pilgrim* (1922) lost the celebrated David and Goliath pantomime, and there were scrappy versions of *Pay Day* (1921) and *A Day's Pleasure* (1922). With all their faults they are still collectable, particularly as they were only issued in small numbers over a short period.

In January 1960, the last Pathéscope film appeared: a Hopalong Cassidy Western, *Doomed Caravan* (1941), in a sound version of seven reels; only three prints were made before the pioneer firm went into liquidation. It is worth mentioning one odd fact regarding this company. Unlike 16mm, which was not only handled by Kodak but any other film laboratory that cared to use the gauge, 9.5mm was exclusive to Pathéscope. Apart from a very few films, every 9.5mm release came from the one firm. By monopolising the gauge, Pathéscope prevented its wider acceptance; had they encouraged other companies in its use, it would in the end have increased rather than diminished its influence on the home movie scene.

For a decade no further 9.5mm movies were printed in Britain. Then in 1970 a couple of British enthusiasts, Paul van Someren and Patrick Moules, keen to carry on the 9.5mm tradition, formed a company called Novascope. They printed 9.5mm films for about five years, until the enterprise could no longer survive the competition of the exciting new releases beginning to appear on Super 8. At first the quality of their results was below that of Pathéscope, later their devoted care led to prints of a most acceptable standard. No features were printed, just a modest range of short subjects, some abridged when Novascope found that collectors would more readily buy a single reel than a full two reel version. Worthwhile Novascope exclusives are *The Tennis Wizard* (from a 16mm Kodascope amber original); a Jack Hoxie Western, *The Desert Rider* (1922); *Belles of Liberty* (1918), a rare Lehrman-Knock Out (LKO) comedy with Monty Banks (credited as Frenchie Bianchi!), and an interesting vintage newsreel, *British Screen News* (1926).

With the disappearance of the British source of 9.5mm, there has been increasing interest in the films issued by Pathé Cinema in France both before and after the Second World War, often frequently longer than the English editions. Not that all these long versions are as impressive as some collectors believe them to be. The editors of the shorter English versions were artful, keeping virtually all of the best scenes in their abridgements and shortening the duller episodes. After the War, Pathé Cinema released a batch of films never issued on any other narrow gauge: a small selection of films produced in the late Twenties by MGM. Titles included *Alias Jimmy Valentine* (1928) with the breezy William Haines; a stylish Norma Shearer vehicle, *After Midnight* (1927), directed with a Continental flourish by Monta Bell; the powerful teaming of John Gilbert and Joan Crawford in *Twelve Miles Out* (1927); and three of Lon Chaney's extraordinary movies (see Part Four).

France has also been the source of some 9.5mm sound films yet to appear elsewhere for collectors. They are essentially for addicts, with dialogue either in French or dubbed into French. Subjects included Capra's Oscar-winning *Mr. Deeds Goes to Town* (1936) as *L'Impossible M. Deeds*; De Sica's *Bicycle Thieves* (1948); two fascinating German sci fi subjects, *F.P.1 Does Not Answer* (1932)—sabotage on a floating airport in the middle of the Atlantic—and *Gold* (1934) with Brigitte Helm—a scientist discovers the secret of manufacturing gold; René Clair's affectionate look back at the early days of the cinema, *Le Silence est d'Or* (1947); and one movie that hardly needs dialogue, *King Kong* (1933).

As a footnote to the 9.5mm story, there is the little known period when Pathé made a brave try at gaining a foothold on the American home movie scene. In 1925, under the name of Pathex Inc., a modified Baby projector and a special range of films were launched on the market in the United States. The subjects included many titles already familiar in the European Pathé lists. In the case of comedy—the predominant *genre* on offer—there were subjects never issued in Europe with stars like Mabel Normand and Theda Bara, featuring in Hal Roach shorts after their careers had plunged. Later when 300 ft. reels began to appear, the French subjects were never released in America. The selection consisted of more comedy and a few B Westerns with such second stringers as Buddy Roosevelt. Just before the final demise of 9.5mm in America, Pathex came out with one unique innovation. In 1931, they introduced sound movies for the home with a Pathé Baby projector coupled to a record player which could be connected to a domestic radio. Using this disc system, similar to Vitaphone, was a sensible move at a time when records gave better audio quality than sound on film. The range of subjects—many from Universal— included twenty-two features, with titles like *Night Ride* (1929) with Edward G. Robinson in his first screen gangster role, thirty-two comedy shorts with sound versions of the Collegians and Sporting Youth, and a host of documentaries. But for all the enterprise of this venture, pre-dating the entry of 16mm sound into the home, it succumbed to the Depression. Pathex was disbanded and 9.5mm became just a memory for American home cinema enthusiasts. Somewhere there must be a lot of those films and discs to be found in the United States.

Part Three

Standard 8 and Super 8— Movies for Millions

In 1929, so "Variety" had it, Wall Street laid an egg! And in 1932, the effects of the Depression and Eastman Kodak hatched 8mm. In the prosperous Twenties with money to burn on fun, 16mm caught on as the latest craze in the United States. In the changed economic climate of the early Thirties, movie making and home shows on 16mm took a back seat, and it was against this background that Eastman Kodak introduced their 8mm gauge, a neat adaptation of 16mm with an eye to economy.

Although, like 16mm, 8mm was movie-making orientated, the home entertainment angle was not overlooked and the Kodascope Library was expanded to accommodate the new gauge. The range of films closely followed the 16mm programme of releases, and many of the films referred to already in the Kodascope 16mm Library were also issued on 8mm during the Thirties. Like the Kodak 16mm prints, the 8mm copies were all on the familiar amber stock. Their quality was outstanding, probably the best prints ever to be made on Standard 8. When the Kodascope Library was finally closed, 8mm prints were sold off, but as there were not so many dealer-operated libraries at the time, more prints were available to private collectors. 8mm amber prints, obviously highly prized collectors' items today, are still occasionally to be found, though perhaps less easily than 16mm prints of the same vintage.

After the Second World War 8mm made slow progress as an entertainment medium. It was still far from being a popular collectors' gauge. During the Fifties, package movie distributors began to increase the number of 8mm releases. In Britain, the firms of Walton and Peak started to include Chaplin and other early comedy subjects in listings that were largely dominated by travel and "interest" movies. In America, Castle increased their scope with more 8mm subjects, subjects that were released in Britain under the GB Movie-Pak label.

At first film collecting on 8mm was inhibited by the rapid rise of television in the Fifties. Why buy films when you can get not dissimilar entertainment free? By the Sixties attitudes had changed. Interest in collecting old films had dramatically increased despite—maybe because of—television. Greater public awareness of the movies' past, film courses at schools and colleges, and the general kindling of interest in motion pictures by television led to a growing army of film buffs anxious to find more opportunities to see the classic movies of the heyday of Hollywood and the European studios. In particular the rise of an "audio-visual generation" of young people, with money to spend, increased the clamour for reprints of the cinema's treasures.

To meet these demands, American distributors like Blackhawk rapidly expanded their range of collectors' movies, and in Britain, on a smaller scale, Walton increased the number of titles in their catalogue with reprints of more early comedy subjects. A newcomer to the package movie scene in the United States was AAP, an offshoot of United Artists, now the owners of much of the Warner Brothers backlog. Their releases specially prepared for 8mm broke new ground with their quality, the use of superimposed titles to avoid wasted screen time, and the introduction of Warner classics like *The Charge of the Light Brigade, They Died with their Boots On, Moby Dick*, and *Noah's Ark* albeit in drastically cut down versions of one reel. Most important of all, AAP was one of the first distributors to release on 8mm magnetic sound.

Early experiments with optical sound on 8mm (the sound carried on a photographically printed soundtrack in the same way as 16mm and 35mm release prints) had never met with much success. The narrow width of the track and its low linear speed gave poor sound reproduction. In 1961, the new technique of striping 8mm film with a narrow strip of magnetic recording material at its edge, and the introduction of projectors capable of handling this magnetic film. resulted in a boost for the scope of the smallest gauge.

Far more significant for the collector was the presentation of a paper to the Society of Motion Picture and Television Engineers in April 1962 by two Eastman Kodak engineers, C. J. Staud and W. T. Hanson Jr. This important paper described a proposed new format for 8mm film. It had long been apparent that as 8mm had evolved from 16mm, the sprocket holes occupied far too large a proportion of the film's area; only 47% of the film was utilised for the picture image. The objective of the new format proposed was to increase the area of the film available for the picture, and at the same time to improve the soundtrack arrangements. After this initial discussion of the new 8mm format, there was a delay until 1965 when the new gauge appeared as the basis of Eastman Kodak's Instamatic moviemaking concept, the redesigned 8mm film being supplied in an easy loading camera cartridge. The new gauge soon became known as Super 8 (from here on in these pages these gauges will be called Super 8 and Standard 8). Heavily advertised on the merits of simplified moviemaking, Super 8 initially made little impact on film collecting, though it should be observed that when Kodak introduced their new gauge it was not only with an eye to fool-proof filming. There was also the intention to provide a gauge less costly than 16mm, but with more potential than the old Standard 8 as a semi-professional film medium capable of improved results on the screen for use in both education and entertainment.

The release of professionally made movies for collectors on the new gauge made slow progress, perhaps because, when Super 8 arrived, Standard 8 was doing well as a collectors' gauge with the issue of many good titles, especially the sound subjects with magnetic tracks. In fact some distributors were decidedly "anti" the new gauge, ignoring it in favour of Standard 8. In part, this antipathy was due to the problems of film damage experienced by libraries using Super 8. The smaller sprocket holes, designed to give a better image area, led to film damage, as did some of the new Super 8 projectors with their automatic threading mechanisms.

After several years of an uneasy situation in which the new gauge became the norm for moviemakers, yet was not accepted for releases of package films, the balance was finally tipped in favour of Super 8. This was primarily due to the introduction of new magnetic sound projectors whose performance outstripped the earlier Standard 8 machines. With these considerations and the lively enthusiasm for sound movies in the home, the benefits of Super 8 could no longer be ignored. But it was not really until 1975, ten years after the introduction of the new gauge, that Super 8 finally superseded the pioneer Standard 8 format once and for all.

From the collector's point of view, the most important phenomenon with Super 8 has been that the major film companies are taking its potentialities far more seriously than they ever did with the other home movie gauges. Films that would never have reached collectors before are now being made available— admittedly in condensed versions—for outright sale. Even allowing for the various shortcomings of some Super 8 prints, the future for Super 8—and the collector—seems brighter than could have been envisaged when the gauge appeared a decade ago.

At the time of writing, in Europe there has been a turn towards optical in place of magnetic sound for Super 8 sound releases. Improvements in printing techniques have made this possible, and the results are impressive. In Europe, optical sound prints are being sold at a lower price than their magnetic equivalents. Optical prints are being made in Britain and many collectors feel that this system offers more consistent sound quality than can be obtained with magnetic sound. Theoretically magnetic soundtracks can provide a superior frequency range, but the need to produce prints quickly in bulk quantities makes it difficult to obtain uniform quality. So far, optical sound on Super 8 has yet to make any impact in the United States.

In many ways, Standard 8 is now as much a collectors' gauge as 9.5mm. In Britain Standard 8 copies of movies are no longer being printed, and in America there is a continuing trend to Super 8. Apart from Milestone, who still release their important range of collectors' movies exclusively on Standard 8, all the other distributors are involved with Super 8. Some companies—for example, Blackhawk—are still printing Standard 8 copies of their releases in parallel with Super 8, but it is hard to believe that this practice will continue indefinitely.

Many of the important Standard 8 releases that began to appear during,

Never seen on the screen, Claude Rains as The Invisible Man *with Gloria Stuart.*

and before, the start of the collecting boom in the early Sixties have fortunately been re-released as Super 8 prints, and will be referred to later. But there have been some titles that have not been converted to the new gauge, usually because the reproduction rights have expired or the sales have not been good enough to justify making further prints. Some of the first Standard 8 magnetic sound releases, now no longer being printed, have become much sought after collectors' items. For example, the AAP UA8 operation resulted in the issue of several mini-versions of Warner Brothers sound movies. An encapsulated *Forty-Second Street* (1933), consisting of abbreviated glimpses of the Warren and Dubin hits "I'm Young and Healthy," with Dick Powell and the chubbily blonde Toby Wing, and the title song "Forty-Second Street," with Powell and Ruby Keeler's hearty hoofing, backed up by Busby Berkeley's well regimented chorines, has become a modern collectors' classic, much in demand. It is puzzling why UA8 did not carry on with the re-issue of short versions of the immensely popular Warner-Busby Berkeley musicals of the Thirties. It must surely have been a profitable sideline.

In Britain, the Midlands firm of Derann issued several classic sound films during the Sixties, selling them outright to collectors. Among these important Standard 8 collectors' items is *The Invisible Man* (1933), with its sympathetic script so true to H. G. Wells's original, surely one of the most underrated of the Universal horror-fantasies and one of James Whale's most brilliant movies. It is interesting that, despite the increased sophistication of process cinematography today, John P. Fulton's pioneer camera trickery still has the power to astonish an audience.

Derann also released a fine print of *Psycho* (1960), the greatest film of Hitchcock's later Hollywood period. Black comedy and genuine horror go hand in hand in this accomplished exercise in audience manipulation. The soundtrack on what was one of the best Standard 8 sound prints to be released truly did justice to Bernard Herrmann's haunting musical score. Neither of these two movies remained long for sale, with the result that they are now as hard to find as Kodascope amber prints.

Powell Films also released several Standard 8 sound titles, now contenders for collectors' classic status. These include Anthony Mann's agreeable Western, *Winchester 73*, starring James Stewart in what was to be the start of a durable partnership with Mann; the Hammer version of *The Phantom of the Opera*, cheaply produced compared with Universal's earlier efforts with Chaney and Rains, but quite an imaginative adaptation of Gaston Leroux' well-worn horror yarn with Herbert Lom as an effective Phantom; and Lewis Milestone's weird, free-wheeling, Depression style musical *Hallelujah I'm A Bum* (1933) with its tuneful score by Rodgers and Hart and attempt to revive the drooping careers of Al Jolson and Harry Langdon.

One of the first firms to release magnetic sound Standard 8 movies, Walton Films issued several titles that have not since appeared on Super 8. *Dark Waters* (1944) has Merle Oberon trapped with a strange family in swamp country, menaced by Thomas Mitchell, uncharacteristically cast as the heavy. The excellent *History Is Made at Night* (1937), directed by Frank Borzage, now recognised as one of Hollywood's finest directorial talents, begins as a light romantic comedy with an unhappily married Jean Arthur falling for a head waiter, Charles Boyer, on the maiden voyage of one of her ship-owner husband's liners. The mood changes when the jealous husband insists that the liner attempts to break the Blue Riband. In fog-bound waters, a Titanic-like situation develops when the ship hits an iceberg, giving this entertaining movie something of the style of a modern day "disaster" picture. With an undistinguished supporting cast, Gary Cooper does battle with a Seminole Indian uprising in Florida swamp country in *Distant Drums* (1951), directed by Raoul Walsh, and one of the few full-length Warner Brothers' features to be released on Standard 8, or Super 8 for that matter.

The two most memorable Walton Standard 8 sound movies, now in the realms of collectors' pieces, were *To Be or Not to Be* and *Stagecoach*. *To Be or Not to Be* (1942) stands out today as one of Lubitsch's most durable comedies. Wickedly laughing at concentration camps and the absurdities of the Nazis right in the middle of the war, its black humour now seems far more potent than the super-patriotic wartime exploits fictionalised on celluloid. It gave Jack

Benny his one worthwhile movie role: "So they call me Concentration Camp Ehrhardt?" is his catchphrase. And the delectable, subtly humorous Carole Lombard is seen at her best in this, her last, movie appearance before her tragic death in an air-crash. Even Lionel Atwill, who could so easily have been given the expected role of a Nazi heavy, has a chance to be funny as a ham actor in Benny's stage company.

Stagecoach (1939) hardly needs an introduction. *The* classic western of all time, this widely enjoyed movie—aptly summed up as *Grand Hotel* on wheels— has something for everyone in its artfully tailored action. It marked a return to westerns for John Ford after ten years on other material, and boosted the career of John Wayne, until then just a B picture cowboy. Although there is an element of corn in the moment when the trumpets of the U.S. cavalry are heard just as it looks as though the beleaguered stagecoach is going to succumb to the Indian attack, one would have to be very hard not to be stirred by this vigorously directed chase and rescue. And apart from the action, there are all those memorable cameos so delightfully played by a cast that crystallises Hollywood's strong team of character supports: Thomas Mitchell, George Bancroft, Donald Meek, Andy Devine, Tom Tyler, Berton Churchill, and John Carradine.

For some time Perry's Movies released exclusively a number of unusual features on Standard 8. As few of these have been converted to Super 8, the original Standard 8 prints can now be considered collectors' items. Subjects in this category include *Bulldog Drummond's Third Round* (1925), an early picturisation of Sapper's essentially Twenties hero, with musical comedy star Jack Buchanan as the man of action; the novelettish *Southern Love* (1924), shot in Austria by Herbert Wilcox and starring Twenties' sex symbol Betty Blythe; *Trapped by the Mormons* (1922), a bizarre, hysterical outburst from British director Harry Parkinson, not uninteresting in its grotesque way as it has the advantage of the beautiful Evelyn Brent caught up in the Mormon trap; Carl Dreyer's *Vampyr* (1931), in mute form but losing little of its power without its soundtrack; James Cruze's "sequel" to *The Covered Wagon, The Pony Express* (1925) with Ricardo Cortez as its Valentino-like hero and George Bancroft as a jovially likeable heavy; Charles Brabin's Art Nouveau version of *Salome* (1923) with the mannered Russian actress Nazimova; and *The Goose Woman* (1925), a powerful movie of character with Clarence Brown extracting a strong performance from Louise Dresser.

During their Standard 8 regime, Perry's Movies also issued a fairly comprehensive range of Griffith titles including one reelers from the American Biograph period as well as the feature *Broken Blossoms* (1919). There was also a wonderful two reeler, *A Day at the Ince Studios* (1922), giving a detailed look at every aspect of production from planning the sets to processing the negatives at Thomas H. Ince's Culver City studio. A fascinating evocation of silent picture making behind the scenes.

The Current Scene—
Super 8 and the Collector

Before looking in detail at the present range of Super 8 movies of especial interest to collectors, several important points must first be made. It is clearly impossible to list every film available—otherwise this survey would be little more than a list of titles. So instead of attempting to refer to every film to be found on the gauge, this is a selective guide to some of the more noteworthy titles exclusive to the distributors mentioned, subjects that may well become the collectors' items of the future particularly if for various reasons they are eventually withdrawn from circulation. (For up-to-date details of the total range of subjects on release, collectors are advised to obtain current catalogues direct from the distributors.)

At the present time a pattern is developing in the releases from all the major distributors of collectors' movies. Along with the silent movies and early talkie classics likely to be purchased by the true film buff, there are also increasing numbers of sound releases in colour, often condensed versions of comparatively recent productions. Some of these titles have collector interest, but mostly they are intended to appeal to the more casual Super 8 projector owner.

The question of the film lengths is often a vexed matter with Super 8 releases. With its standard reel capacity of 200 ft., a full Super 8 reel has a running time of 15 minutes at 16 fps, 13 minutes at 18 fps, and 10 minutes at 24 fps (10% shorter in running time than a Standard 8 200 ft. reel). Many purchasers of Super 8 films assume not unreasonably that a 200 ft. reel will contain approximately 200 ft. of film. But in practice, a film advertised as being on a 200 ft. reel may well contain no more than 150 ft. of film with a running time of $7\frac{1}{2}$ minutes at sound speed. This is obviously an irritation for collectors, a situation that could be avoided easily if all distributors followed the example of the few and stated a movie's true footage—or running time.

Walton Sound and Film Services Ltd.
The oldest existing British distributor of Super 8 movies, Walton started releasing Standard 8 films way back in the Fifties, their first success being an enterprising coverage of the Coronation of Queen Elizabeth II. With their

Will Hay (left) and his comic foils, Moore Marriott and Graham Moffatt, who appeared in several classic British comedies of the Thirties.

comprehensive range of movies for collectors they are a major force on the Super 8 scene today.

Classic movies from the heyday of the British studios are an important element of the Walton repertoire. There is Michael Powell's impressive reconstruction of a wartime incident, *The Battle of the River Plate* (1956); the stylish romantic melodrama, *The Man in Grey* (1943), featuring the cream of the British stars of the time; the important *Brief Encounter* (1945), scripted by Noël Coward and directed by David Lean; and Hitchcock's delightful *The Lady Vanishes* (1938), happily blending thrills, humour and suspense with consummate skill.

Walton have done an invaluable service to connoisseurs of British film humour by reviving *Oh! Mr. Porter* (1937) and *Ask A Policeman* (1939), starring music-hall comic Will Hay. A comedy classic directed with just the right touch by Frenchman Marcel Varnel, *Oh! Mr. Porter's* lasting appeal with collectors depends on its hilarious teaming of Will Hay with cheeky fat boy Graham Moffat and snaggle-toothed old Moore Marriott, together with a strong vein of nostalgia provided by the steam locomotives it features. And there are also two popular comedy hits of the Fifties: *Genevieve* (1953), notable for its vintage cars and a superb comedy performance by beautiful Kay Kendall; and *Doctor in the House* (1954), the first and best of a long series.

All these features are released in full-length versions with slight cuts, to fit into a standard 8 or 10 reel format. The footage given on each reel is generous, so that a collector will get what he expects: 200 ft. of film on a reel. In addition to the full versions, there are also two reel abridgements of all these features. In view of the problems inherent in the drastic cutting of sound movies, the results are remarkably effective (the versions of *The Lady Vanishes* and *Brief Encounter* are notably well done), making excellent souvenirs for collectors. By issuing these two reel (400 ft.) short versions, Walton pioneered the digest technique adopted more recently by Columbia for their Super 8 releases.

An indication that considerable exposure on TV can enhance rather than diminish the demand for certain movies by collectors is the successful release by Walton of a batch of ten MGM Tom and Jerry cartoons in colour, all from prime years when Fred Quimby was their producer.

Walton are the British distributors of the shorts and features that Laurel and Hardy made for Hal Roach. Some of these have been pruned, and the range of titles is far from complete. *The Music Box* (1932) has lost a reel, though the neatly timed, percussive dance the team perform to the music of the pianola has been left intact. *Big Business* (1929), the ultimate "reciprocal destruction" movie, has been cut to one reel, and some of the features have sequences missing. British Laurel and Hardy aficionados naturally regret that the only versions of their comedies available should be abridged.

Of Walton's small batch of Harold Lloyd's silent comedies, *Captain Kidd's Kids*, *High Hopes* (originally *Never Weaken*), and *Courtship Ahoy* (originally *All Aboard*) were subjects once released by Kodascope. Only *Assailing The Sultan*, an extract from *A Sailor Made Man* (1921)—Harold rescues Mildred Davies from a harem—is not to be found elsewhere.

Among the many documentaries from Walton are *Elizabethan Express*, made by British Transport Films in the Fifties, an outstanding movie having much in common with the classic *Night Mail; The Flying Scotsman Runs Again*, a BBC TV film covering a commemorative trip by the famous steam locomotive; and several railway films of the pre-war years before nationalisation from the British Transport archives.

Recently Walton have begun to concentrate on colour sound movies. So far, the most important of these is *Witchfinder General* (1968), with Vincent Price scoring as the sadistic witch-hunter at the time of the English Civil War, directed by Michael Reeves whose early death robbed the British cinema of a major talent. Other titles in colour include *The Curse of the Crimson Altar* (1968), one of the last movies to star the grand old man of horror, Boris Karloff, and an extract from *One Million Years B.C.* (1966), with shapely Raquel Welch and some brilliant animation of prehistoric monsters by Ray Harryhausen.

Mountain Films Ltd.

In sheer quantity of subjects, Mountain have become the largest British distributor. Apart from being the agents for the American Columbia and Ken

Films releases, they have a range of Super 8 sound features covering subjects all the way from sexploitation sensations to titles like *Body and Soul* (1947), one of the most powerful of all movies on the fight game.

The Mountain features of especial importance for collectors are: Raoul Walsh's *The Naked and the Dead* (1958), based on Norman Mailer's best seller; Jand Russell—"mean, moody, and magnificent"—in *The Outlaw* (pioneer sex Western of 1943); Fritz Lang's 1952 encounters with two of the screen's greatest sex symbols in *Clash by Night* (Marilyn Monroe) and *Rancho Notorious* (Marlene Dietrich). And there are several cut-price movies from PRC with plenty of interest for addicts: *Gangs Inc.* (1940), an early Alan Ladd vehicle; *The Devil Bat* (1940)—Bela Lugosi planning a weird revenge on business associates who have betrayed him; and *Misbehaving Husbands* (1940)—middle-aged Harry Langdon having a fair stab at modifying his baby face comic style to the needs of domestic situation comedy.

Even more collectable features from Mountain are *Murder Inc.* (also known as *The Enforcer*) (1951), starring Humphrey Bogart as a crusading DA nailing a murder ring, one of the few Warner Brothers' features to be released on Super 8, and the last properly integrated Marx Brothers' comedy, *A Night in Casablanca* (1946) which, while not as notable as their early work, is quite a funny movie—a fair souvenir considering it is their only feature on Super 8.

Most of the Mountain versions of features have been edited to a nominal

Terror on Skull Island. Fay Wray and Bruce Cabot in King Kong.

eight reels, some of which are shorter than the standard 200 ft. Abridged versions in the manner of the popular two reel digest format are not issued, but there are some reasonably well chosen extracts from certain of the titles.

Mountain also release the three great, skyscraper scaling, "thrill comedy" climaxes from Harold Lloyd comedies: *Never Say Die* (from *Never Weaken*), *Safety Last* (1923), and *Height of Madness* (from the early talkie, *Feet First*, 1930). And there is also the charming silent short, one of the free-wheeling Griffith Park comedies, *Spring Fever*. Also hiding among the less distinguished silent shorts from Mountain are two rarities, both from Chaplin's First National period in the form of several short extracts: *The Last Tram Home* (from *Pay Day*, 1922), and *A Dog's Life* (1918).

In 1976, Mountain negotiated the Super 8 rights for the whole of the RKO Radio library of over 700 titles, thus opening up the possibility of collectors being able to add copies of *King Kong* (1933), *Citizen Kane* (1940), and the evergreen Astaire-Rogers musicals of the Thirties, to their private archives.

Breakspear Films

Unique amongst the British distributors of collectors' movies is Breakspear Films, a one-man operation by an enthusiast, John Cunningham. A collector himself, Mr. Cunningham has selected subjects from his own library of rare 35mm prints and personally made direct 8mm master negatives from these high quality originals. The result is copies of an unusually high standard—each print is a collectors' item in itself, the purchaser privileged in sharing Mr. Cunningham's enjoyment of his unique collection.

The releases have been on Standard 8 with subjects including *The School Teacher and the Waif* (1912), a likeable example of D. W. Griffith's work for Biograph with Mary Pickford excellent as a mixed-up teenager; the Fatty Arbuckle Keystone comedy, *The Water Dog* (1914), demonstrating the advanced editing techniques—many camera set-ups and complex intercutting—used by Mack Sennett, far more noteworthy than his comedy construction; the Russian Starevich's *The Grasshopper and the Ant* (shown before the Czar in 1913!), and a Vitagraph human drama, *An Old Man's Love Story* (c1912). Recently Mr. Cunningham has been working on the preparation of Super 8 prints of the rare George M. Cohan feature, *The Seven Keys to Baldplate* (1920).

Other additions to the Breakspear Super 8 range are to be a compilation made by Mr. Cunningham of the cinema at the turn of the century, and prints of the rare Chaplin Keystone *A Busy Day* (1914), with Charlie in drag as angry housewife.

Fletcher Films Ltd.

Fletcher are newcomers on the Super 8 collecting scene in Britain. Many of their releases are familiar material—re-titled versions of silent Laurel and Hardy comedies, cartoons, and re-prints of Kodascope subjects. It is in the actuality department that Fletcher have released exclusive footage, a run of pre-war and wartime annual news reviews produced by Gaumont British.

Gaumont British News had a style and pace that kept it one step ahead of the other newsreels in Britain. Produced by ex-feature film director Castleton Knight, these newsreels used fancy opticals and fast cutting to give a sense of urgency and drama to events, and the commentary by the inimitable voice of E. V. H. Emmett matched the visuals. The annual news round-ups with their signature tune composed by Louis Levy, conductor of the Gaumont British Symphony Orchestra (instant nostalgia for any British film buff over forty!), may not always be an accurate reflection of their times—they were often flippant and naive, not even above manipulating their visuals—but they survive well because they made news entertaining.

Powell Film Distributors Ltd.
The carefully selected range of titles from Powell Films contains quite a high proportion of "collector material". Will Hay is to be found as the shifty governor of a prison treating the convicts as if he were the headmaster of a boys' school

Kenneth More in A Night to Remember.

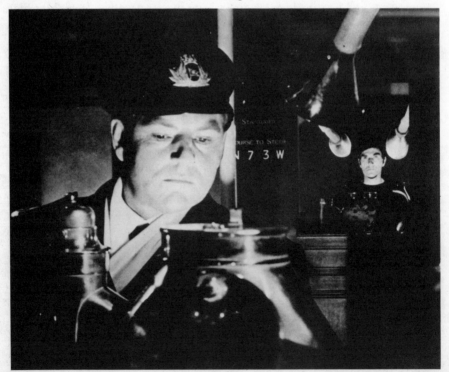

in *Convict 99* (1938), another comedy classic brightly directed by Marcel Varnel. More vintage British comedy is seen in *The Ghost Train* (1940), starring British radio comic Arthur Askey as an end-of-the-pier funster helping to solve the mystery in this wartime adaptation of the much filmed stage melodrama. Forestalling the disaster movies of a couple of decades later, with a creditable attempt at reconstructing the sinking of the Titanic, is *A Night to Remember* (1958), soberly recounting the events surrounding the loss of the liner, its documentary realism laced with a few human cameos.

Powell also exclusively released several major American movies including the outstanding Robert Youngson compilation, *Days of Thrills and Laughter* (1961), combining well-chosen comedy moments (the Charley Chase item is an absolute gem, and the Monty Banks entry, *Play Safe*, seen almost in its entirety, is an astonishing piece of stunt comedy rivalling Keaton at his best), with cliff-hanging high-spots from serials of the Twenties. Powell have issued some of the self-contained comedy segments as shorts, a useful service for collectors not wanting the complete feature.

Other important titles include Max Ophuls subtle, romantic *Letter from an Unknown Woman* (1948), Fritz Lang's interesting big city thriller, *While The City Sleeps* (1956) with a strong cast and a suspenseful story-line, Orson Welles' rarely-seen, controversial version of *Macbeth* (1948)—reputedly quickly made using old Western sets on the Republic lot, George Cukor's *A Double Life* (1948), mingling real life murder with a Shakespearian actor's obsession, Ronald Colman winning an Oscar for his role as the demented player, Fred Astaire marking time in *Second Chorus* (1940), hardly in the same league as the memorable RKO musicals, but with the compensation of seeing Fred dance with the sparkling Paulette Goddard, and Bud Abbott and Lou Costello doing their version of a Christmas pantomime in *Jack and the Beanstalk* (1952).

Three of John Wayne's best known movies are a part of the Powell programme. *The Quiet Man* (1952), a perfect example of the style of John Ford, made on location in Ireland using his "stock company," has Wayne as the ex-heavyweight champ who returns home to find a wife. The Ford Western *Rio Grande* (1950) stars Wayne in a typical role: a tough U.S. Cavalry colonel at war with the Apaches. He is even tougher as the seasoned sergeant training Marines for a dangerous mission in *Sands of Iwo Jima* (1949), directed by veteran Allan Dwan.

Powell have obtained the Super 8 rights for the release of historic newsreels and up to date "specials" from the British Movietone News Library. One true collectors' item is *British Movietone Newsreel No. 1* (June 1929), of considerable interest with its primitive handling of the new medium of sound used on location for the direct recording of the perennial Trooping of the Colour and the Derby. A complete run of annual News Reviews from 1934—including the war years—makes up an archive of the major events of four decades of Twentieth century history.

Perry's Movies Ltd.

As has already been mentioned, this company was a major supplier of Standard 8 prints of silent movies for British collectors. For some time after the introduction of Super 8, Perry's resisted changing over to the new gauge. Then eventually—like other British distributors—they bowed to the inevitable and switched completely to releasing their movies on Super 8. At the same time, realising that there was an upsurge of interest in sound movies, they changed their releasing policy to concentrate on the issue of full length and two reel digest versions of sound subjects.

The Stars Look Down (1939), one of the few British movies of the Thirties to take an unpatronising look at the working class, is based on A. J. Cronin's best seller. Certainly Carol Reed's first major success, this movie reasonably well succeeds in painting a realistic picture of life in a mining community. Convincing special effects of the flooding and holocaust in the mining disaster bear favourable comparison with Pabst's earlier *Kamaradschaft*, and in an era where happy endings were the rule it risks a downbeat finale with all the miners perishing in a blocked pit. Breaking another rule, it has a "heroine" (excellently played by Margaret Lockwood) who is completely unsympathetic. The rest of its fine cast is headed by Michael Redgrave as the idealistic miner turned school teacher.

Another unusual movie—an early British talkie—from Perry's is *Dick Turpin* (1933). Starring Victor McLaglen who came over from Hollywood to appear as the Robin Hood of highwaymen, this is a museum piece. The acting style—McLaglen apart—is a return to the stilted costume movies made by the smaller British studios in the silent days. Its use of sound is primitive even by the standards of the early Thirties: the background music is no more than a pot-pourri of popular classics played in the manner of the accompaniment provided by a pit orchestra in the silent cinemas, and the hoof beats of Black Bess sound as if they were dubbed from the clippety clop of a couple of coconut shells! But despite the dated technique this traditional British adventure yarn still stands up well, helped immensely by McLaglen's definitive portrait of the legendary highwayman.

Foreign Correspondent (1940), Hitchcock's second American movie, hits on themes he already used in his British movies. An American newspaperman (Joel McCrea) is unwittingly involved with assassination (the Hitchcock touch: a high angle shot of umbrellas bobbing out of the way marks out the escape route of the assassin), gets deeper embroiled with the kidnapping of a diplomat (Hitchcock suspense: eavesdropping on Nazi plotters in a Dutch windmill, McCrea's raincoat gets caught in the revolving cogs of the mill . . .), and finally uncovers the Nazi masquerading as head of an international peace mission (remember how the master spy in *The 39 Steps* was a respected Scottish laird?). In addition to the feature, a well arranged two reel digest preserves some of the best scenes from this better than average Hitchcock thriller.

Amongst the collectors' items in Perry's short subject section, *The Devil*'s *Work* stands out. This is a Pathé Frères' trick film of 1905, directed by Gaston Velle, clearly a rival of Méliès but with ideas of his own. A conjuror in skeleton make-up brings up close to the camera three bottles filled with liquid and then turns to reveal three tiny women dancing in them. Later he builds up a set of building blocks, and on the wall thus constructed there appears a woman with a dog—in action! The intricate special effects and close ups of this astounding reel are topped by the fact that it is in colour—laboriously hand tinted. The Super 8 version reproduces this effectively, making it a fascinating collectors' piece.

Derann Film Services

Apart from running one of the largest Super 8 film libraries in the world, this Midlands firm is also a major distributor of movies for sale to collectors, specialising in Super 8 sound. Although some of the subjects they handle are perhaps not of interest to the serious collector—B horror movies for example—there are some well chosen titles in their programme of releases. Robert Siodmak's excellent thriller *The Dark Mirror* (1946) has much of the dark, expressionist quality of UFA psychological dramas—not altogether surprisingly because Siodmak had started his career with UFA in 1929 as a writer and film editor. Olivia de Havilland is given a field day as two sisters—one good, one bad—and much of the suspense is bound up with identifying just which sister is responsible for the murder of a young man, Siodmak cleverly keeping the audience in some doubt as to which girl is a schizophrenic. Quietly patient Lew Ayres—one time Dr. Kildare—plays the psychiatrist hero who finally tricks the real murderess into revealing her guilt.

The two Max Fleischer full length colour cartoons, *Gulliver's Travels* (1939) and *Hoppity Goes to Town* (1941), are outstanding examples from the classic years of animation. *Gulliver's Travels*, somewhat weak on the characterisation of Gulliver through the use of "rotoscoping" (a method of tracing live action invented by Fleischer), does nevertheless have some brilliant animation; the scenes of the Lilliputians moving the giant Gulliver with all kinds of gadgets is inventive and ingenious and the characters of the two warring kings, Little and Bombo, are amusingly portrayed. Another strong point is the catchy musical score by Leo Robin.

Little creatures predominate in *Hoppity Goes to Town*, which is better animated than *Gulliver* though still lacking the Disney spark of genius for characterisation. Fleischer's penchant for mechanical gadgetry and sharply drawn comparisons between the insect and human worlds are well used in this Capra-like story of a little guy (Hoppity the grasshopper) optimistically trying to help the insect population threatened by the building of a skyscraper, suffering pitfalls and disaster until he finally leads the insects to a penthouse garden. Again Fleischer's feature scores with a hummable line-up of musical hits by Hoagy Carmichael and Frank Loesser.

REPUBLIC PICTURES PRESENT

The Amazing Exploits of a Modern Miracle Man!

ADVENTURES OF CAPTAIN MARVEL

12 EPISODE SERIAL

TOM TYLER
FRANK COGHLAN JNR.
WILLIAM BENEDICT · LOUISE CURRIE

REPUBLIC PICTURES

Directed by WILLIAM WITNEY   Associate Producer HIRAM S. BROWN Jnr.

REPUBLIC PICTURES CORPORATION Herbert J. Yates, President · DISTRIBUTED for REPUBLIC PICTURES INTERNATIONAL INC. (Great Britain)

All twelve chapters of Captain Marvel have been released on Super 8.

From these Fleischer features one reel extracts have been prepared: the "All's Well" number from *Gulliver* with the Lilliputians transporting the slumbering Gulliver and the "Katydid" number from *Hoppity* with the brilliantly animated Electric Dance by Hoppity make up two perfectly self-contained reels from these cartoon classics. (In America, the feature length versions of these two movies are handled by Niles Films.)

The best of all the Republic serials—maybe one of the best serials of all time—*The Adventures of Captain Marvel* (1941) is issued in 12 episodes. Benefiting from some superior special effects—Tom Tyler's power dives through the air as Captain Marvel look surprisingly convincing—and far-fetched action in the true serial tradition, this collectable chapterplay is also to be found as a two reel extract (actually the complete first episode plus the pay-off from Chapter Two).

Norman Wisdom, British comic of the Fifties, is something of an acquired taste. Originally greeted as a second Chaplin by over-enthusiastic critics on the look-out for a super-comic at the time, his brand of humour now seems too self-indulgent for many screen comedy buffs. In particular, his calculated attempts at pathos are completely resistible, though when he gets a good gag situation he can be very funny. One of his best comedies is his earliest, *Trouble in Store* (1953), which milks gags from the sure-fire background of a department store, already well used by Chaplin and the Marx Brothers as a setting for laughter. Excellent support from his talented foil Jerry Desmonde, and the delightful Margaret Rutherford as a compulsive shop-lifter, helps to make this movie a hit.

From back in the Thirties comes another museum piece, *Off the Dole* (1934), the second comedy to star the immensely popular North Country comic, George Formby. Produced in Manchester to cash in on his rise to fame on gramophone records as a singer of risqué songs accompanied by his vigorous ukelele strumming, this is sound film-making at its most primitive: every shot is a ten minute take! But by immortalising George Formby's singing and unpretentious humour, the cinematic crudity of this movie is blithely over-looked by Formby's followers (there is still an active fan club devoted to his records and movies!).

Castle Films

First name on the American home movie scene after Kodak was Castle Films, a company already releasing 8mm and 16mm single reclers before World War II. In fact, the Castle concept of package movies set the pattern for other rival home movie operations. Apart from the news reviews and some See magazine reels, the pre-war releases are of little interest.

Castle releases today still consist of single reel reductions or extracts from features originally produced by Universal and Paramount. Generally the single reel format is too restrictive for anything other than a trailer-like set of high-lights from the chosen features. From the earlier Castle subjects, *The Bride of Frankenstein* (1935)—an extract from the film's finale rather than a con-densation—is justifiably popular since it retains all the excitement of Colin Clive and Ernest Thesiger's giving of life to Elsa Lanchester and her rejection of Boris Karloff, with Franz Waxman's haunting music in the background. Other titles cover James Whale's further classic, *The Invisible Man* (1933), his original *Frankenstein* (1931), Tod Browning's classic *Dracula* (1931) with Bela Lugosi as the definitive vampire, and a number of lesser monster movies from Universal City. One rather good one is the Lionel Atwill–Lon Chaney Jr. sci fi horror movie, *Man Made Monster* (1941), with the eerily glowing Lon (mad doctor Lionel has charged him with electricity) wandering through the countryside.

Castle have made extensive use of the movies Abbott and Costello starred in for Universal, including their meetings with *Frankenstein, Dr. Jekyll and Mr. Hyde, The Mummy*, and the *Keystone Cops*. These Abbott and Costello one reelers come over reasonably well, but the W. C. Fields extracts from *It's a Gift* (1934), *If I Had a Million* (1932) and *The Old Fashioned Way* (1934), and the sequences from the Marx Brothers' Paramount classics, *Horse Feathers* (1932)

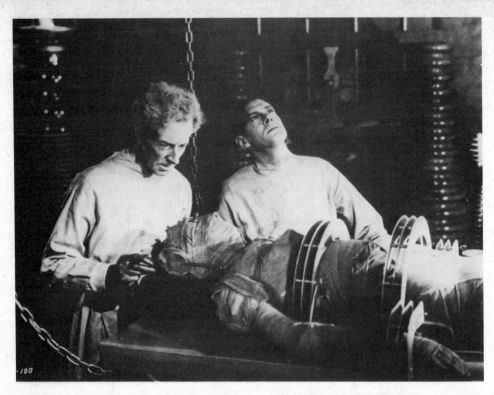

*Above, making a monster's mate — Ernest Thesiger and Colin Clive
in* The Bride of Frankenstein. *Below, Bela Lugosi in* Dracula.

and *Duck Soup* (1933), are a rather inadequate souvenir of the work of some of comedy's immortals.

Coming more up to date, Castle have now released one reel round-ups of highlights from Hitchcock's *Psycho* (1960)—the murder in the shower and the killing of the detective on the stairs—and the film he returned to England to make, *Frenzy* (1972), in colour.

Cinema Eight

This company is somewhat different to the other distributors of collectors' movies mentioned in this survey. Until recently it has been selling Standard 8, Super 8, and 16mm movies from most of the other major distributors, offering them at attractively discounted prices. It is interesting to find that originally this firm only handled the 8mm gauges, but now stocks 16mm versions of films, where available, because schools—who have become important customers for vintage movies—are still geared to 16mm rather than the newer formats.

Cinema Eight has now broadened its activities to include its own exclusive releases in Super 8 sound, as well as still selling—at a discount—the products of the other distributors. There is no doubt that some of the titles will grab the attention of film buffs on the lookout for rare items on Super 8.

From the Hollywood Poverty Row studio of Monogram (once a joke, but now weaving its own peculiar spell over addicted movie collectors) comes *Spotlight Scandals* (1943), a musical about vaudevillians with veteran comics Billy Gilbert and Frank Fay—and even silent clown prince Harry Langdon. Also from Monogram, Cinema Eight are releasing nine comedies featuring the East Side Kids. A spin-off from *Dead End*, this rough and ready series used some of the Dead End Kid originals (Leo Gorcey and Huntz Hall, for example) and others including Ernie Morrison—Sunshine Sammy of Hal Roach silents (Africa in the early 9.5mm shorts).

More in the classic mould are twenty-four of the original two reelers from Chaplin's Keystone, Essanay and Mutual periods, each converted to run correctly at sound speed ("time-processed" in Cinema Eight's description) together with a full orchestral score and sound effects.

Cinema Eight have also the Super 8 rights of two of the most interesting movies, both produced in Britain, of Boris Karloff's later years. *The Haunted Strangler* (1958), a variation on the Dr. Jekyll and Mr. Hyde theme, has Karloff as an author investigating a murder of the past and then discovering that he himself is the psychopath responsible for the crime. His strong performance, backed by Anthony Dawson—usually a suave villain, but here a Scotland Yard detective—and Jean Kent as a spirited cabaret singer, makes this an absorbing and out of the rut thriller. More disturbing, because its roots are in reality rather than fantasy, is *Corridors of Blood* (1958). Here Karloff is a dedicated surgeon before the discovery of anaesthesia, working on the relief of pain but developing an addiction to the drugs he uses in his experiments, who becomes the dupe of a gang of bodysnatchers. Quite powerfully handled by director Robert Day, with an eye to the horrific possibilities of clinical detail, this is a meaty melodrama allowing Karloff full rein for his distinctive acting talents.

Columbia Pictures

More than any other consideration of film collecting at the time of writing, one aspect has come to the fore—and that is a clear demand for movies with sound. There is a good potential for the sale of sound features to collectors, but for many enthusiasts the cost of buying a feature outweighs other considerations. So taking a more positive line with regard to film collecting than most of the other major Hollywood production companies, Columbia have arrived at a working compromise, the release of specially condensed "Viewers' Digest" versions of a cross section of their fifty-year-old backlog of features. These condensations are in the 400 ft. reel format, with a running time of 20 minutes.

Despite the considerable loss of footage in this drastic editing, many of the shortened movies so far released have been handled with remarkable skill. Where there are obvious gaps in the storyline, a voice-over commentary fills in the story to cover the loss of continuity. The whole idea works well: *On The Waterfront* (1954) is quite brilliantly handled such that it appears as a smoothly narrated story; without reference to the original it is hard to see just what is missing. One less attractive aspect of Columbia's treatment has been the insertion of "editorial comments," like the moment in *The Commandos Strike At Dawn* (1942) when the commentator chips in with the statement "Seen here as the German officer is Lloyd Bridges in one of his first major screen roles," completely destroying the dramatic impact of the action that follows. But this is a minor criticism of what has been the most promising development in making a major studio's movies available—albeit in shortened form—to collectors. While there are some dyed-in-the-wool film buffs who resent any cutting of a movie, for the majority the technique works extremely well. In effect it is a return to the Pathéscope idea of two reel cut-downs of silent features.

Amongst the Columbia Viewers' Digest two reelers are a good selection of their classics from the Thirties: Frank Capra's *Miracle Woman* (1931), *It Happened One Night* (1934), *Mr. Deeds Goes To Town* (1936), and *Mr. Smith Goes To Washington* (1939), Howard Hawks' *Twentieth Century* (1934) and *Only Angels Have Wings* (1939), and Leo McCarey's *The Awful Truth* (1937). On the musical side they have revived the two movies Fred Astaire made with Rita Hayworth, Forties' dream girl—*You'll Never Get Rich* (1941) and *You Were Never Lovelier* (1942)—and Hayworth partnering Gene Kelly in *Cover Girl* (1944), as well as the immensely popular—but cinematically negligible—*The Jolson Story* (1946) and *Jolson Sings Again* (1949).

Meeting the demand for a different breed of collector to those who seek out vintage silent and sound movies, Columbia have included a sampling in sound and colour from some of their more recent forays into blockbuster

Two Columbia releases. Above, Gary Cooper in Mr. Deeds Goes to Town. *Below, Glenn Ford and Rita Hayworth in* Gilda, *a superior Forties melodrama.*

territory. Catering for every taste, they have also released a proportion of **B** picture programmers in the Viewers' Digest output.

From the collector of vintage movies point of view, the reappearance from Columbia's vaults of many long forgotten two reel comedies of the Thirties is splendid news. Apart from the Three Stooges, who were their resident comics, the Columbia short subject department became the last resort of comedians who had seen better days. Charley Chase, Buster Keaton, and Harry Langdon, three comic masters of the silent era, all did a stint with Columbia. Occasionally amongst the generally rather faded attempts at recapturing their former glories, these comedians succeeded in turning out a gem. For example, Charley Chase's *Rattling Romeo* (1939)—Charley wins a prize and buys a beaten-up car—is a pleasant return to the standards of his earlier work. But Keaton's silent masterpieces were such works of genius that his Columbia shorts hardly seem to be the comedies of the same man. All the Columbia shorts are released in their original form without any cutting.

Walt Disney Productions

Unlike other important Hollywood producers, Walt Disney have shrewdly set their sights on the public they understand best—the family audience. And there is little doubt that in terms of the undemanding pleasure they have provided for the screen they have few rivals. Disney are also unusual in that they handle within their own organisation the preparation and release of Super 8 copies of a selection of their movies. This has enabled them to ensure that the best master material is available, so that their prints are generally of excellent quality, setting standards that other distributors aspire to.

Although a good selection of the classic Disney shorts have been released, they are only in the form of mute silent films. This is a great pity. The whole of Walt Disney's basic conception of animated cartoons, the very reason for his original phenomenal success with Mickey Mouse, revolves around the close integration of sound and picture. Viewing the mute prints of such gems as *The Tortoise and the Hare* (1935) from the Silly Symphony era, and the two Mickey Mouse subjects, *Clock Cleaners* (1937) and *Lonesome Ghosts* (1937), one is constantly aware of the missing dimension of sound. And what is the Silly Symphony masterpiece of 1933, *The Three Little Pigs* without the song that made it a hit of the Depression years: "Who's Afraid of the Big Wolf?"

The sound titles that have been released are extracts from the popular feature length cartoons. It is possible to argue with the choice of scenes that have been selected for these releases, but on the whole they come over extremely well with representative sequences from such features as *Snow White and The Seven Dwarfs* (1937), *Pinocchio* (1939), *Cinderella* (1950), *Alice in Wonderland* (1951) and the recent *Robin Hood* (1973). The extract from *The Jungle Book* (1967) is especially choice, to all appearances like a completely self-contained short subject with its hilarious encounter between Mowgli and the Ape King Louie, and the catchy song and dance routine with Louie and music mad Baloo.

Griggs Moviedrome

Claiming to be the second oldest firm in the United States supplying silent and early sound prints on 8mm and 16mm to discerning collectors, Griggs Movie-drome is the amalgamation of the enterprise of the late John Griggs, an actor and film collector, and the long established Essex Film Club. All the laboratory work on the prints from this company is guaranteed, and defective prints are replaced, a factor that gives collectors added confidence when ordering prints.

The range of subjects is impressive. There are the W. S. Hart Westerns, *Hell's Hinges* (1916), an important early work which Hart directed and acted in for Thomas H. Ince, and *Tumbleweeds* (1925) with its celebrated—and exciting—Cherokee Strip land-race and a spoken prologue by W. S. Hart in person to introduce the talkie re-issue. Several of Douglas Fairbanks's major silent features including *The Mark of Zorro* (1920), *The Black Pirate* (1926), and *The Thief of Baghdad* (1923) are available in either Standard 8 or 16mm prints, or both.

Buster Keaton is to be found in *Steamboat Bill Jr.* (1928), the sissy son of a riverboat captain coming up trumps in a tornado, and in his early short master-piece, *Cops* (1922), with its nightmarish hordes of policemen. A good cross-section of the work of D. W. Griffith on both shorts and features ranges from the first of the last minute rescue melodramas, *The Lonely Villa* (1909), to the first Griffith sound film, *Abraham Lincoln* (1930). John Barrymore, surviving on film as one of the cinema's most enjoyable actors, is in the ex-Kodascope print of *Beau Brummel* (1925), co-starring with the lovely youthful Mary Astor, and *Tempest* (1927), its action set in Russia just before the Revolution.

Foolish Wives (1922), Erich von Stroheim's extra-ordinary work combining the banal with scenes whose power still survives, and Henry King's moving, suspenseful, and sensitive *Tolable David* (1921), beating D. W. Griffith at his own game, represent peaks of Hollywood's silent output.

Griggs Moviedrome are also strong on European classics (see Chapter 4). Especially noteworthy are their versions of the outstanding Russian movies: Eisenstein's *Battleship Potemkin* (1925), *Ten Days that Shook the World* (1927), and the sound masterpieces, *Alexander Nevsky* (1938) and *Ivan The Terrible* (1942–46). Some of these are as yet only available as 16mm prints. An offbeat Russian movie is *Bed and Sofa* (1927), a human comedy frankly handling such controversial subjects as abortion, housing shortages, and women's rights. Way ahead of its time, it resembles a modern problem movie.

In the realm of sound, there is on 16mm only at present Bette Davis in her first great acting triumph, *Of Human Bondage* (1934), a movie long thought to be lost until a 16mm print was discovered, and *The Front Page* (1931), directed by Lewis Milestone with Pat O'Brien and Adolphe Menjou rattling out Hecht and MacArthur's gritty dialogue.

Milestone Movies Corporation

With an exciting line-up of true movie classics, Milestone have only concentrated on the Standard 8 format. However, they now have immediate plans to release on Super 8.

The long-lost F. W. Murnau feature for Fox, *City Girl* (1929) has appeared, fortunately intact with all the footage reported to have been scrapped and re-shot by another director during the hiatus of the switch to talkies. De Mille's influential drama of 1915, *The Cheat*, *Spangles* (a programmer from 1926 starring the attractive Marion Nixon as a bare-back circus rider), and *Lucky Devil* (1925), culminating in a comedy-with-thrills car race, an ex-Kodascope subject featuring Richard Dix falling for the lovely Esther Ralston, are all the latest releases from this important American distributor.

Other Milestone titles include: *Down to the Sea in Ships* (1923) with a youthful Clara Bow; John Barrymore's tongue-in-cheek portrayal of François Villon, *The Beloved Rogue* (1927), a superb spectacle with comedy and stunning settings by William Cameron Menzies; and the glorious Louise Brooks, most striking of all silent female stars with her beautiful smile, in *Pandora's Box* (1929); Keaton's masterpiece, *The General* (1927); Erich von Stroheim's first major hit, *Blind Husbands* (1918); a bizarre crime story by Tod Browning, *The White Tiger* (1923), with Wallace Beery; Josef von Sternberg's first movie, *The Salvation Hunters* (1925); and a number of ex-Kodascope titles like *Manhandled* (1925), with Gloria Swanson in a down-to-earth role; Reginald Denny's action comedy, *The Kentucky Derby* (1922); Mal St. Clair's romantic comedy, *Are Parents People?* (1925); and *Orchids and Ermine* (1927), perfectly preserving the period of Scott Fitzgerald with flapper Colleen Moore and tiny Mickey Rooney. Milestone are also strong on European classics (see Part Four), recently adding to their range of subjects a full ten reel version of Dupont's lavish *Moulin Rouge* (1928) made at Elstree for BIP.

Niles Film Products Inc.

Specialising in Super 8 sound shorts and features, this company has an important range of titles not to be found elsewhere. The shorts consist of complete comedies and cartoons, and two reel condensations of features. Amongst the shorts are *The Dentist* (1932), most robustly vulgar of the quartet W. C. Fields made for Mack Sennett; the three spectacularly animated Popeye subjects featuring the spinach-gobbling sailor's meetings with *Sindbad the Sailor* (1936), *Ali Baba* (1937) and *Aladdin and his Wonderful Lamp* (1939); and there are early appearances by Bing Crosby and Lucille Ball.

The two reel condensations include the sci fi classic, *Things to Come* (1936), excitingly directed with a distinctive visual style by William Cameron

Colleen Moore.

Menzies. Largely taken from the early part of this famous Alexander Korda production, Niles's short version contains the memorable air raid scenes which uncannily predict the feelings in Britain three years later.

Bela Lugosi, the Hungarian with the strong accent and piercing eyes, was so closely associated with his appearance as Dracula that he spent the rest of his career trying to live it down. Type cast in mediocre B movies, where his name on the credits was sufficient to lure gullible audiences into believing they were going to get something truly shocking on the screen, he got few good opportunities for his menacing manner. Niles have done Lugosi some justice with a two reel digest of *Human Monster* (1939), a rare excursion by a British studio into the realms of horror. With Lugosi disguised as the principal of an institute for the blind, this curiously disturbing movie is more realistically horrific than its Hollywood counterparts. Lugosi's finest hour—actually 73 minutes—on the screen is in *White Zombie* (1932), majestically sinister as the necromancer using zombies to work his Haitian sugar mills. A once only hit for its director Victor Halperin, this unique horror movie is finely tuned to extract the maximum impact from its eery scenes. Niles have the full feature available on Super 8.

Amongst the other titles in Niles's roster of full-length features there are three British classics of the Thirties. Hitchcock's *The 39 Steps* (1935), memorable for its teaming of wrongfully accused Robert Donat with the reluctant Madeleine Carroll, and its artful blending of humour and thrills; Hitchcock's less well known *Secret Agent* (1936) with John Gielgud and a curly haired Peter Lorre; and *Transatlantic Tunnel* (1935), a re-make of a German sci fi movie, with Richard Dix fighting all odds to build an undersea tunnel linking England with America.

From Hollywood there are several outstanding features: Archie Mayo's *Svengali* (1931), John Barrymore's acting as the evil genius, Anton Grot's incredible sets, and Barney McGill's deep focus photography—anticipating the effects of *Citizen Kane*—all making it an early talkie classic; Frank Borzage's faithful version of Hemingway's *A Farewell to Arms* (1932), with fine work from Gary Cooper and Helen Hayes; and one of the best of the Thirties' "crazy comedies" genre, *My Man Godfrey* (1936), launching Carole Lombard as an outstanding comedienne and Mischa Auer as the looniest of comics.

Thunderbird Films

A major American distributor of Super 8 prints with their own in-plant processing and pre-production laboratory, Thunderbird are particularly strong on important American silent stars and offbeat subjects from Europe. Most of their releases are at present on Standard 8 and 16mm as well as Super 8.

American stars include Rudolph Valentino in two of his best movies, *The Eagle* (1925) and *Son of The Sheik* (1926), both proving that he was more than an empty male sex-symbol with his tongue-in-cheek sense of fun and adventure; Mary Pickford, still in teenage roles long after she was a woman in her twenties, in the exciting melodrama, *Sparrows* (1926), helping a band of orphans escape from the farm where they are held as slave labour (its high spot had the children's terrifying experience of having to pass through quicksands and a crocodile-infested swamp); Twenties' "It" girl, Clara Bow, whose winsome personality still shines on the screen in a typical dime novel adaptation, *Dancing Mothers* (1926); and even rarer, one of the few features made by the sensational escapologist, Harry Houdini in *The Man From Beyond* (1921).

Carl Dreyer's intensely moving *The Passion of Joan of Arc* (1928), with one of the great acting peaks of the silent cinema—Falconetti's unsurpassed, heart-rending performance as Joan—heads several features from Europe. Another great piece of silent playing is that of Vera Baranovskaia in the Soviet movie, *Mother* (1926), directed by V. Pudovkin putting all his theories on montage into practice. And Arthur Robison's German *Warning Shadows* (1922), made without sub-titles, constantly fascinates with a subtler use of expressionism than that in most of the German silents, at times reminding one of Ingmar Bergman's work, while Alfred Hitchcock's rarely seen *Easy Virtue* (1927) shows what the young British director made of a silent movie of a Noël Coward play.

Thunderbird have something unique for collectors with their coverage of

Valentino and Vilma Banky in The Son of the Sheik.

the Avant Garde, the Underground movies of the Twenties. Erno Metzner's *Uberfall* (1929) uses optical distortion to suggest mental states, *Le Ballet Mécanique* (1925) has hypnotically repeated images and strange editing by abstract painter Fernand Léger, and *Ghosts Before Breakfast* (1928) humorously employs stop-motion to show everyday objects (hats, coats, cups, etc.) rebelling against their daily routine.

Joris Iven's *Rain* (1931) is a perfect little study of shower in Amsterdam (a model for all amateur moviemakers) and *Blood of a Poet* (1935) has many of the personal symbols of the artistic virtuoso Jean Cocteau which were to turn up again in his other eccentric features.

Recently Thunderbird have released one of the first of the Famous Players films—*The Count of Monte Cristo* (1912), reputed to be the Earliest American feature in six reels, in a version prepared from paper prints held in the Library of Congress. In addition to the silent release, there is also a sound print with an organ score and effects. Griffith's *The Birth of a Nation* (1914) has also been released in a number of versions, some with sound and some with coloured sections reproducing the tinted effects in the original prints.

Blackhawk Films Inc.

Towering above all the distributors of silent films for collectors is Blackhawk, whose massive range of vintage movies contains riches exceeding those of the original Kodascope and Pathéscope catalogues. Enjoying an excellent reputation for the quality of their prints and the care with which they are presented, Blackhawk have been providing not only re-prints of old favourites but also have discovered and released copies of lesser known rarities of unusual interest. Many of the Blackhawk releases are in three versions—Standard 8, Super 8, and 16mm—making this company one of the best legitimate sources of 16mm vintage prints, though as with other distributors Super 8 is becoming more and more important.

Blackhawk always introduce their silent movies with comprehensive "programme notes" commenting on the film's background, stars, and director. Some collectors apparently find these introductory titles tedious, though others rightly consider that they show Blackhawk care about their movies sufficiently to put them in historical perspective. The answer for those who dislike these introductions is to cut them out, since Blackhawk invariably retain the original main titles as well. (Incidentally, titles are important to collectors, who always feel cheated if the original titles in the movies they collect are missing, or have been replaced with fresh titles incompatible with the period of the subject. Today, under pressure from collectors, most distributors endeavour to retain original titles, even if they have to be shortened. Many of the two reel digest versions have their titles intact. In Britain, collectors are also pleased to see the British Board of Film Censors' certificate at the start of a movie.)

Such are the treasures of the Blackhawk archive it is only possible to give a cross-section of the scope of the subjects. The reader is referred to the company's catalogue for the full range of titles. Blackhawk is a veritable store-house of comedy and one of the most important sections is their comprehensive listing of Laurel and Hardy—the most complete available—with everything from their initial partnership in *Do Detectives Think?* (1927) to sound features like *Blockheads* (1938). And there are a few of the movies of Stan Laurel and Oliver Hardy in solo appearances including Oliver Hardy's supporting roles in the shorts of other Hal Roach contract comics.

Other Hal Roach comedians represented include Charley Chase in some of his two reelers, silent and sound, including the blithely absurd *Now We'll Tell One* (1933), Charley wearing a strange belt causing him to do crazy things by remote control; Our Gang (the Little Rascals) in a complete festival of their comedies; and Edgar Kennedy and Stuart Erwin in the "one off" Roach comedy, *A Pair of Tights* (1928), as a couple of tight wads taking out two girls on the cheap—Marion Byron's business with the ice cream cones making this a classic

Stan Laurel at work with Oliver Hardy in The Finishing Touch.

of comedy construction. Unfortunately for collectors in Britain and other parts of the world, this invaluable source of Hal Roach comedies is denied to them: Blackhawk's rights in these subjects only permits their sale in the United States and Canada.

Like Laurel and Hardy, Charlie Chaplin is lavishly represented by virtually all his shorts together with a complete print of his masterpiece, *The Gold Rush* (1925), a release only available for sale in the United States. Harold Lloyd is inadequately covered—because of copyright restrictions on his later films—by only five of his early shorts (the best is *Haunted Spooks*, 1920), but Harry Langdon, one of the great silent pantomimists, is commemorated by some of the hilarious series of shorts he made for Mack Sennett. Sennett, whose studio was the training school for many comic talents, has all phases of his silent output available. But not all the fun came from the famous: there are the sleepers too, like *Air Pockets* (1924) featuring the unknown Lige Conley, a hilarious little movie with a wild torrent of gags.

Away from comedy, the work of D. W. Griffith receives worthy treatment with many of his American Biograph one reelers from *The Adventures of Dollie* (1908) onwards to *The Birth of a Nation* (1915) and *Intolerance* (1916). Major silent stars—Douglas Fairbanks, Lon Chaney, Rudolph Valentino, William S.

Hart, Tom Mix—are represented by several titles a piece, and the ladies of the cliff hangers—Pearl White, Helen Holmes, and Arlene Pretty—appear in episodes from their chapter plays. Silent features from Hollywood include such rarities as *Traffic in Souls* (1913), George Loane Tucker's movie that showed sex on the screen paid—in a big way (it recouped eighty times its production costs at the box office!). And *Block Signal* (1926), one among many railroad melodramas, proves that the lure of steam locomotives is a strong collector interest, with the young and pretty Jean Arthur as an added attraction.

Foreign features figure importantly with several of the UFA classics (see Part Four), Pudovkin's *The End of St. Petersburg* (1927)—available with a full orchestra musical score—and René Clair's odd little trick film *The Crazy Ray* (1923). From Britain there are Alexander Korda's productions: *The Private Life of Henry VIII* (1933), and *The Rise of Catherine the Great* (1934), and the absorbing documentary account of submarine warfare in the First World War, *Q Ships* (1928). Amongst the offbeat short offerings there is the Clarendon Company of Croydon's intrepid naval hero in *Lt. Rose and the Hidden Treasure* (1912), and Starevich's charming fable, *The Voice of the Nightingale* (1923), reproduced in colour from an original Prizmacolor print.

Blackhawk are particularly strong in their range of vintage documentaries and actualities. Robert Flaherty's perennially fresh *Nanook of the North* (1922), and his last film *Louisiana Story* (1948), together with Walter Ruttmann's superb *Berlin: The Symphony of a Great City* (1927), Pare Lorentz' *The Plow that Broke the Plains* (1936), the disaster story of the "Dust Bowl," and Arne Sucksdorff's evocation of Stockholm—comparable with Ruttmann's picture of Berlin—*Symphony of a City* (1948), are all just a part of a fine archive of documentary classics.

Recently Blackhawk have released selected items from the Fox Movietone library, samplings from newsreels and "specials" like the original sound newsreel of Lindbergh's flight and return in "The Spirit of St. Louis" in 1927, with on-the-spot synch. sound of the occasion. And there is a wonderful collectors' piece, an interview with Sir Arthur Conan Doyle (1927)—long believed to be lost—in which the grand old man describes how he came to create the immortal Sherlock Holmes and then goes on to discuss his committed belief in the after-life—a rare—and intensely moving—record of a Victorian legend.

Part Four

The Mechanics of Collecting

The Projector

Almost any well made projector will satisfy a movie enthusiast if all he wants to do is show the children on the beach. But the choice of a suitable projector by a film collector needs more care. Before looking at some of the machines of special interest for collectors, it is useful to understand the question of projection speed and how it effects the reproduction of silent films.

It was the Lumière Brothers, responsible for a number of shrewd fundamental decisions in the design of their Cinématographe, who calculated that the best shooting speed for silent films was 16 frames per second. As time went on, and the movie camera became more widely used, this shooting speed was only used as a working basis, never strictly adhered to. It couldn't be. All professional cameras in the silent era were hand-cranked and cameramen had their own ideas as to the best shooting speed.

Projectionists tended to show films at a speed faster than the taking rate, and cinematographers at the major studios began to shoot at speeds more closely corresponding to the projection speeds. Thus the shooting speed of many American silent movies of the Twenties were much faster than 16 fps—sometimes as high as 24 fps, in fact. So the range of shooting speeds found in the silent films bought by collectors is a wide one. Comedies were usually shot at 16 fps (with speeded-up shots at 8 fps, or lower—for comic effect, of course), as were silent newsreel and actualities. Early dramas—those from D. W. Griffith, for example—were at 16 fps and so were most of the silent features from the continent. But later American silent features could vary from 20 to 24 fps, and some of the British features (those from BIP, for example) appear to have been shot at speeds higher than 16 fps.

All this makes a projector with continuously variable speeds an essential for the keen collector of vintage silent movies. He can then see these films as they were intended to be viewed, avoiding the absurdities of the over-fast projection of silent movies as seen on TV and in cinema re-issues. Most modern Super 8 silent projectors have fixed-speed induction motors set to run the machine at 18 fps—the "official" shooting speed for amateur silent movie making. This speed provides a compromise for the projection of vintage silent movies shot between 16 and 20 fps, but is obviously not ideal for getting the best results on the screen. Far better to use a Super 8 machine with a truly variable speed control for projecting vintage silents. Such machines are available, though tending to become far less common than fixed speed projectors.

With the collection of sound movies on Super 8 growing in popularity, more and more collectors are obtaining sound projectors. These again are fixed speed machines, designed to operate at 18 fps for silent movies and 24 fps for sound. Projecting a silent movie on a sound projector is a compromise; usually the 18 fps setting works best, though in some cases an American silent movie will project better at 24 fps. The keen collector may well want to own a separate variable-speed, silent Super 8 projector for showing his silent vintage prints.

Other considerations influencing the choice of a Super 8 collector's projector include the question of whether he will be giving shows to larger audiences than the family circle, requiring a machine with a faster lens and more powerful lighting than one designed purely for home use. And if he is interested in sound, he may well be looking to the future and will want a machine capable of handling optical as well as magnetic sound tracks. Also for more professional results, there is one current projector—the Japanese Elmo ST-1200—which will take 800 ft. spools, thus reducing the number of reel changes when projecting a full length movie in the same way as 16mm.

The choice of a 16mm projector does not represent much of a problem. Most modern machines can be adjusted to operate at fixed speeds of 16 and 24 fps, and are all capable of professional results on the screen. Once again, the keen collector may prefer to own a second, variable speed projector for his silent movies. Here there is a good choice, as there were many 16mm projectors made in the past solely for silent movies. There are a couple of snags with these older projectors, though. Their light output may be below acceptable modern standards, and possibly they will not be able to accommodate 1,600 ft. spools. Amongst the older 16mm silent projectors, those made by Eastman Kodak and Bell and Howell are worth the keen collector's attention. Built like the proverbial tank, they are strong enough to outlive a lifetime, collectors' items in their own right.

There are a number of dual gauge machines—both sound and silent—able to project Super and Standard 8 movies by means of a simple changeover of parts. These clearly make it possible for a collector with a library of Standard 8 movies to carry on showing these, as well as being able to increase his scope by collecting Super 8 prints. With the demise of Standard 8, there are many second-hand Standard 8 only projectors being offered at reasonable prices, though not many of these are particularly desirable as collectors' machines. Some are poorly designed and constructed, with inferior lenses and lighting. Worth looking for, both as excellent performers and as collectors' pieces, are the early Standard 8 Eumig, Cirse, and Silma projectors while the Kodak Sound 8 is a particularly well-built sound machine. Probably the most highly regarded of all Standard 8 projectors is the Paillard Bolex M8R, a classic of precision and good design. With its variable speed control, and its fine lens, it gives the best possible results from Standard 8 silent movies.

The enthusiast who builds up a collection of 9.5mm notched reels will

The most advanced of the Pathé "notched" title projectors, the Lux.

have to look for a secondhand machine to project his films. Apart from its feeble lighting, the original Pathé Baby projector in good condition is capable of giving fair results with the notched films it was designed for. The later, more powerful, Pathé Lux was also designed to project both the short 30 and 60 ft. notched films as well as 300 ft. reels. With its built-in motor, it works completely automatically with the notched films, performing extremely well. For the best results from the early notched prints there is only one machine capable of providing screen images for larger audiences than in the home; it is the Paillard Bolex PA, giving a performance comparable with 16mm projectors of its time. Rejuvinated with one of the new tungsten halogen lamps, the results are even more satisfactory.

9.5mm projectors are still being made in France, but although the modern machines are able to give results of 16mm quality on the screen, they do not necessarily handle early Pathéscope prints satisfactorily. One machine made for many years that is popular with 9.5mm collectors is the Specto. Its strong construction, trouble-free operation, and basically simple design make it extremely effective for use in the home and in small halls. It will not operate automatically with notched titles.

There were never many projectors made for 9.5mm sound, so the choice is restricted. The original Pathé Vox is still much favoured by enthusiasts. Brought up to modern standards with tungsten halogen lighting, a photo-diode in place of the photo-electric cell, and a modern transistor amplifier, it gives excellent results. Later machines that are popular include the Pathé Pax, though the more widely available British made Pathé Son is by no means as well constructed as the French models.

The choice of projectors for 28mm and 17.5mm is even more restricted. Original 28mm KOK machines with their hand-cranked dynamo to power the lighting can sometimes be found, and a mains model without the dynamo has occasionally appeared, but these are rarities, as much collectors' items as the films they show. 17.5mm Pathéscope Home Talkie projectors of the Thirties are rare. Even rarer is the powerful Pathé Super Rural. Introduced shortly before the folding of 17.5mm sound in Britain, it gave results of theatre quality.

Selecting a screen needs some thought. If the projector is of lower power— a Pathé Baby, for example—and the last ounce of light has to be squeezed from it, a silver or beaded screen is essential. Even better is the superb Kodak Ektalite screen, though this is an expensive luxury for projecting 30 ft. 9.5mm prints on. For the normal Super 8 machine where there is plenty of light available, a non-directional plain white screen is to be preferred so that all members of the audience will see an image of equal brightness. Apart from permanent installations, it is sensible to have a screen complete with its own integral stand.

Projection Technique—Giving a Show

When presenting a show at home, or to a club audience, there are several simple rules to follow if a good impression is to be given of a collector's films. Firstly, always set the projector and screen up well before the audience arrive. This makes it possible to find mains electric sockets, to hide away cables (and avoid accidents), and to place the speaker (if it is a sound show) in the best position near the screen. It is helpful to have a small pilot lamp near the projector to avoid having to turn on the room lights between every reel change. If it is possible to control the room lighting with one of the thyristor dimmers that are now available, the effect is far more professional than suddenly switching the lights on and off.

Before projecting the programme it is sensible to check that all the films have been rewound, and multi-reel features have their parts ready in the correct order. After the films have been shown, they should never be rewound until the programme is finished. It is preferable that they should be rewound slowly on a separate rewinder after the show.

One vital accessory is a spare projector lamp. Nothing is more embarrassing than to have a lamp blow part way through an important show—and not to have a spare. So it is essential to have a spare lamp of the correct type ready in case of a lamp failure. A simple accessory, guaranteed to improve the presentation of a show of collectors' movies, is a piece of white card about 8 inches square! This is held in front of the lens after the lamp has been switched on, to prevent all the flashes and synch. numbers on a movie's leader from reaching the screen. It is better than using the lamp switch, as the defocussed image on the card indicates to the operator the precise moment when the titles are to appear on the screen. Similarly at the end of a reel, the projector beam can be blocked off immediately after the end credit titles appear. A good projectionist never shows a white screen!

In the days of the silent cinema, films were never viewed in silence. There was always an orchestra or pianist to provide a fitting musical background to the pictures on the screen. In just the same way, a show of vintage silent movies is enhanced if there is a well chosen musical accompaniment to underline the action. The ideal is a live pianist in sympathy with silent movies, with a flair for extemporising suitable themes. In fact, the combination of a classic silent movie and an inventive pianist following the action can be one of the most satisfying of all audio-visual experiences.

Failing having a live pianist, suitable music can be taped before the show and run in approximate synchronisation with story on the screen. Classical orchestral music works well with drama (but over familiar themes should be avoided), and Twenties-style dance music and jazz is an obvious choice for comedy. But it should be remembered that if such recorded music is to be used at a public show, a licence will have to be obtained from the appropriate organisation.

One promising development on the provision of music for silent movies, avoiding all the trouble of selecting suitable pieces, is the appearance of "sound" versions of famous silent films, with magnetic sound tracks of specially arranged music. Now that there are increasing numbers of collectors owning sound projectors, this technique for enhancing the impact of silent movies is likely to become the pattern for many future releases.

Preserving the Collection

A film only has value while it is projectable. A film which has its sprocket holes damaged through careless projection, or its emulsion badly scratched through rough handling, is going to have little value regardless of how rare it may once have been.

Film is a fragile material, consisting of a thin layer of emulsion, gelatine carrying a silver—or colour—image coated on a base of cellulose acetate, and can be easily damaged in a variety of ways. The emulsion will be scratched in the projector gate if gelatine debris is allowed to build up to form a hard "corn" on the runners; similarly a sticking roller in the film path will cause emulsion damage. Scratching may occur if the take-up spool fails to revolve smoothly and snatches the film or—even worse—fails to revolve at all, so that the film spills all over the floor. Rewinding too fast on the projector can also cause scratching, and it should be noted that pulling the end of a losely rewound film to tighten it on the spool—known as "cinching"—is another sure way of scratching the emulsion.

Sprocket hole damage can be caused by failing to ensure that there are adequate film loops above and below the gate, and a sticking feed spool will almost certainly cause sprocket hole tearing. There is also a danger of serious sprocket hole damage at the beginning of a film if it is fed into a self-threading 16mm or Super 8 projector without first splicing on a length of the special thick base leader recommended for these machines.

The need to splice on leaders, to remove damaged sections, and to repair sprocket holes makes a film splicer an indispensable accessory. There are two types of splicer for Standard and Super 8 and 16mm—tape or cement. The tape splicer is particularly useful for sprocket hole repairs. It uses either prepared splicing patches or, in the case of the excellent Italian made C.I.R. splicer, punches the sprocket holes out of the polyester tape supplied for making joins and patching torn sprocket holes. Tape splicing is essential for joining the polyester base release prints that are now beginning to appear.

For the non-technically minded, a cement splicer is not as convenient to use as a tape splicer; the emulsion has to be scraped from one end of the film before a join can be made, as it is in effect a welding of the film base. Cement splicing is cheap—all that is needed is a splicer and a bottle of cement to make hundreds of splices. There are plenty of cement splicers on the market but it is a false economy to buy one of the cheaper models. An accurate instrument is essentials, and the Eumig, the Kollmatic (with its built-in motor driven scraper), and the professional Premier are all well designed cement splicers giving perfect joins.

Cement splicing has to be used for 9.5mm and the obsolete gauges. Incidentally, it is occasionally difficult to get a join in an old print to "stick." In such cases it is worth trying different makes of cement to find the type that works best with a particular reel of vintage film.

Film damage can be avoided on the new films bought by a collector, but the vintage prints he may find are almost bound to have damaged sections, or suffer from some of the other effects of age on the emulsion and film base. In case of long sections of torn sprocket holes, these should be cut out completely. If this leaves a portion of a shot that is too short on the screen, the undamaged remainder should be cut out, too. Where there is the odd damaged sprocket hole or two, these can be patched with a tape splicer using polyester patches or tape. 9.5mm can be patched using either prepared "perforation patches" or do-it-yourself patches punched from a strip of clear film.

If a film on Standard 8, Super 8, or 16mm is sufficiently rare to justify the expense, a reversal duplicate can be made of the damaged section—the laboratory using the undamaged side of the sprocket holes to run the film through the

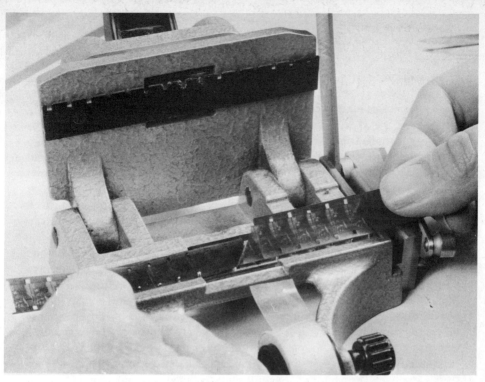

Above, repairing a 16mm film on a C.I.R. tape splicer.
Below, patching a 9.5mm film with damaged sprocket holes.

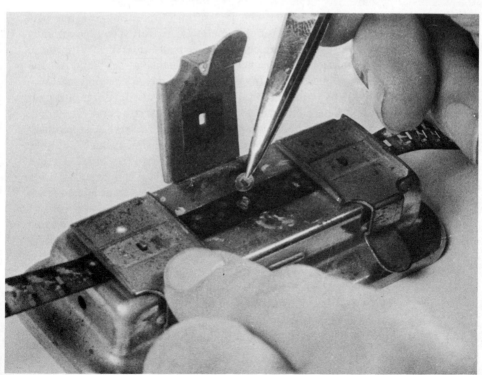

printing machine. It is also possible to get laboratory treatment for scratches on the film base of 16mm to minimise the effects of wear on an old print.

Although cellulose acetate safety film does not turn unstable like 35mm nitrate base, it is affected by a loss of plasticisers, becoming brittle with age. This can cause sprocket holes to split at their corners, and as time goes on these brittle films will be unprojectable because the splits will eventually extend across the whole width of the film. This is particularly disastrous with 9.5mm where the sprocket holes are wider than in 16mm and the film narrower. For this reason 9.5mm prints should be carefully examined with a magnifier to check for evidence of sprocket hole splitting. Obviously the value of a film will drop considerably if it has deteriorated in this way.

Another effect of shrinkage is for a film to "bow" across its width on 9.5mm, or to develop a permanent warp on 16mm. Either condition makes it difficult to keep the film flat in the projector gate, or even to project it at all. Often these films will also not wind up properly on the take-up spool. One remedy that is worth trying is to wind the film inside out interleaved with a roll of recently processed new stock, rather like a swiss roll, then to put the combined film in a can with a pad soaked in a proprietary humidifier, and seal it with tape. With luck, after several weeks· storage the film may be flatter. Some collectors have their films given Permafilm treatment to improve their smooth running through the projector, but this is not always effective with shrunken early films.

Films that have been stored in damp conditions—in a garage or loft, for example—may show another fault. This is "crazing," appearing as a fine network of lines etched into the emulsion. Sometimes there are also random star-like marks on the emulsion's surface. There is really no remedy for these faults. Emulsion is an animal gelatine subject to fungicidal attack—and it is the effect of the growth of microscopic fungi that causes these damaging marks.

To avoid troubles of this kind with new prints—or old prints, for that matter—they should be stored in metal or plastic cans in a moderately cool room with a temperature no higher than 65°F. Films must *never* be stored near a warm radiator. In the past, humidor cans, with a special pad which had to be moistened with humidifying solution, were popular. This form of storage can sometimes give an old print improved flexibility, thought it is doubtful whether new prints stored in the way described above—in a temperate climate with normal humidity—really need humidor cans.

Special cans for Super 8 and 16mm are quite expensive if you have a large collection. So some collectors, with large numbers of reels to store, buy sturdy, square cardboard containers which are both cheap and practical. An even less expensive solution to the storage problem is to get hold of 16mm—or even 35mm—empty raw stock cans from a film laboratory. These not only look right but offer excellent protection for their contents.

The title of the film in each container should be clearly labelled on its outside. Dymo tape is ideal for this, and by using different colours for various types of subject some kind of order can be given to a private archive. Keen collectors like to keep a log on each film—either in the can or in a separate card index. This indicates the history of the print, where it was acquired, its condition, repair work carried out, the number of times and dates on which it has been screened. Not only does this add to the fun of owning a collection, it also soon shows which films are really worth keeping.

Cans and cardboard boxes offer films good protection but look unsightly. However attractive a movie may be on the screen, a spool of film is a spool of film! For collectors who want to make their movies look more presentable as a library, there are good looking—but expensive—film storage systems with elegantly designed book-form containers suitable for a library shelf.

It is an interesting side-light on the mentality of collectors that many enthusiasts like to keep vintage 9.5mm or 16mm movies in their original containers despite their shortcomings for storage. Old yellow Kodak and blue, circular Pathéscope boxes have as much a lure for collectors as the films they contain. Even if they put the reels in modern cans the odds are they will carefully preserve the old boxes!

Collectors' Organisations and Publications

Most collectors begin as loners, drawn to old movies for a variety of reasons. Some collectors continue to enjoy their hobby as a solitary pursuit, but after a while many enthusiasts begin to feel the urge to join an organisation that will provide a focus for their hobby. Apart from the benefit of being able to share one's interests with others, joining a club can be a spur to collecting, making possible useful contacts and the chance of mutually advantageous exchanges.

The longest established society for film collectors in the world is the Vintage Film Circle. A British society founded in 1956, well before the expansion of 8mm collecting, by a small group of collectors mainly interested in old 9.5mm prints, it has increased its scope over the years to include all the collectors' gauges. With a membership of film buffs from all over the world, it can lay claim to being the most international of all the collectors' organisations.

The members are kept in touch with the Circle's activities by "Flickers," the journal of the VFC which appears about twice a year. This is an entertaining forum for reminiscences on old movies, and reviews of collectors' films. The complete set of all the editions of "Flickers" since 1956 makes a unique review of the changing face of film collecting over two decades.

Every month a group of VFC members living in the London area meet in a spacious restaurant room above the bar of a City pub. The meetings are primarily shows of rare subjects from members' own archives, part of an annual printed programme sent to all Circle members within reach of London. But they are more than just cinema shows, they are the chance for enthusiasts to chat about collecting, to boast about their latest finds—and to mourn the films that got away! Even more to the point the members are there to sell and swap old movies. In fact, there is often so much of this socialising that it is hard to find time to screen any films!

The most remarkable of all the magazines devoted to film collecting is "Classic Film Collector," a quarterly journal edited and published in America by its energetic founder, Samuel K. Rubin. Sam started his publication at the start of the Sixties under the name of "8mm Collector." Its name was changed and its scope expanded when collectors on other gauges took an interest in this unique magazine. It now covers all the gauges, carrying a regular column on 9.5mm topics. Consisting of a tabloid newspaper format running into as many as eighty information packed pages per issue, it has the space to combine solid information with trivia. It is an indispensable source of material on all aspects of collecting.

A spin-off from the "Classic Film Collector" is the organisation called the Society for Cinephiles which holds an annual four day long convention, the Cinecon, for collectors throughout America and the world. At the last Cinecon, the eleventh, held in Hollywood, collectors came from Canada, England, Denmark, and Australia, as well as from all over the United States. Films are shown in abundance, stalls have films for sale, and collectors have films for exchange, making this an important annual event in every serious collector's diary. In addition to the actual film content of the Cinecons, famous stars from the Golden Age of Hollywood are invited to attend and reminisce on their experiences, face to face with a new audience that has only got to know them through revivals on the collectors' gauges.

A notable one-man enterprise in Britain, a service to 9.5mm sound film collectors, is that offered by Maurice Trace. About three times a year he publishes his magazine, "9.5mm Sound News," an essentially amateur publication, in the best sense of the word, managing to pack into its few pages a considerable amount of information not to be found elsewhere. This is truly a labour of love by its generous editor, who offers to supply it free of charge to all collectors providing stamped addressed envelopes.

In addition to this magazine, Maurice Trace has compiled a definitive listing of every 9.5mm sound film issued by Pathéscope in Britain, together with original production details, date of release, etc. Recently he has further extended his useful range of publications for the specialist collector with a guide to 250 dramas issued by Pathéscope in 9.5mm silent versions. Similar in detail to the sound film listing, this is an invaluable guide to any collector of 9.5mm movies.

In 1974, a young British collector, Steven Herbert, formed the Film Collectors' Society, an organisation designed to put collectors in touch with other film buffs having similar interests largely through the medium of a quarterly magazine, "Film Collectors' News." While not as lavish as the American "Classic Film Collector", this is an estimable little journal, extremely well produced and full of facts on all the collectors' gauges, the latest issue containing an entry on 28mm. One of the main advantages of this publication circulating among collectors is that, like the other collectors' magazines, it prints sale and wants advertisements at no charge to subscribers.

Taking a leaf from the Society for Cinephiles and their annual Cinecon in the States, the FCS had the objective of holding a yearly convention for British collectors. In 1976 this ambition became a reality with a well attended day-long convention at a private London cinema. Every collector's gauge was represented from 28mm (with the projection of some rare movies on the Pathé KOK), 17.5mm (with several fascinating early sound prints shown on the Pathéscope

Home Talkie), 16mm amber prints, 9.5mm notched and sound films, all the way to the latest Super 8 sound and colour movies. In conjunction with "Super 8 Collector' magazine, an award was given to the best package movie of the year, based on content and print quality. The 1976 choice was Columbia's two reel Viewers' Digest version of the Oscar winner of 1953, *On the Waterfront*. The first British Collectors' Convention was a sweeping success, undoubtedly to become an annual event rivalling the Cinecon.

1975 saw the introduction of two new magazines of importance for collectors—one in Britain, the other in America. "Super 8 Collector" is designed to provide the newest gauge's aficionados with unbiased reviews on the content and quality of the bewildering number of Super 8 prints now reaching the collecting scene. Edited and published in Britain by Paul van Someren, a film buff of wide interests (his was the brain behind the Novascope 9.5mm film printing operation), this magazine provides short factual reviews, fresh and hard hitting in style. Occasional articles on technical problems and the overseas collecting scene make for a valuable service to the keen Super 8 collector.

The most professional in appearance of all the magazines devoted to movie collecting is the newest addition, "Private Screenings," which only started in April 1975. Edited by John Cawley, Jr. and published irregularly in California, this is a worthy addition to the coverage of the collecting hobby. A mixture of short articles on popular film subjects (Laurel and Hardy, and Batman, have received treatment so far), film reviews (not unlike those in "Super 8 Collector"), and news of collecting at home and abroad, make up its contents. Previous editions have dealt in depth with Disney's releases on Super 8, and the controversial subject of film piracy.

Part Five

Chaplin's Mutual Dozen

By any standards the twelve comedies Charles Chaplin made under his Mutual contract in 1916–1917 represent the most sustained output of comedy in movie history. In Chaplin's own words, "Fulfilling the Mutual contract, I suppose, was the happiest period of my career." And it has been a fluke of good fortune that this happy series of comedies have been widely available to the film collector. Such is their popularity they have probably been the first films that many collectors have cut their teeth on. Unlike the later Chaplin films, under his personal control and shrewdly re-released at optimum occasions, these remarkable movies have been part of the stock in trade of most home movie distributors both today and in the earliest days of 8mm, 9.5mm, and 16mm.

The Mutual dozen had a particularly successful combination of talents. Apart from Chaplin in peak form, there's the beautiful, cool Edna Purviance, complementing Charlie so perfectly with her sense of humour and first class timing. There is the splendid troupe of comic stock players, many of whom play several roles in the same film. Long, lanky Albert Austin, dolefully watching his clock being dissected in *The Pawnshop*, beefy Henry Bergman playing in drag on occasion, memorably in *The Rink*, and Leo White, the excitable Frenchman or crazy count, are among the perfect supporting cast. Towering over all these characters is Eric Campbell, the screen's greatest comic heavy. There is little doubt that this wonderful adversary for Charlie is one of the most important ingredients for the success of the Mutuals. Campbell's playing has more to it than meets the eye. His villains could have been total brutes—and therefore not very funny—or they could have been the usual run of forgettable adversaries that abound in screen comedy. He's a brute alright, but he's a brute with style—and a sense of humour—who is worthy of playing alongside Charlie's own acting brilliance. None of Chaplin's other villains were to match the mighty Eric Campbell, and none of the silent comedians were ever to find an adversary to compare with the burly Scotsman who had once played for the D'Oyly Carte Opera Company. He was in a class of his own.

Chaplin was well established by the time he made his Mutual comedies. A rapid rise to fame in the Keystone films he made for Mack Sennett marked him out as the leader of the field. Many of these Keystone comedies are available in Super 8 copies of varying quality. They have their moments, and some of the subjects are popular with collectors. Chaplin is far from being the sentimental clown in these films, he's rough and tough. But the crude knockabout of such Keystones as *His Trysting Place* where he gets an ironing board broken over his

Edna Purviance.

The screen's greatest comic heavy, Eric Campbell, in The Rink.

Chaplin's relief at finding marriage has its snags — from the end of Keystone's The Face on the Bar-Room Floor.

*Charlie with Mabel
Normand in Keystone's*
A Gentleman of Nerve.

head by shrewish Mabel Normand and uses an old man's beard as a table napkin, and *A Gentleman of Nerve*, where he makes Mack Swain suffer with violent kicks on the bottom—and in the stomach!—can still raise a few laughs.

After Chaplin's move to Essanay, violent slapstick was toned down and the tramp character began to emerge. While not in the same class as the later Mutual comedies, some of the Essanay shorts are well regarded by collectors, like *The Champion* (sparring partner Charlie wins a fight with a horseshoe in his glove), *A Woman* (Charlie, superb, in drag flirts with his girl's lecherous father), *A Night at the Show* (Charlie in two roles, a drunk man about town in the stalls, a rowdy in the gallery, reduces a music hall to a shambles), *The Bank* (Charlie dreams he captures some bank robbers and wins Edna), and *Police* (Charlie burgles a house, but decides to go straight when the girl who lives there turns out to be Edna [the police are satirised as ineffectual fops]).

In February 1916, after some furious bidding for Chaplin by the movie producers, he signed up with the Mutual Company to make twelve comedies at the unprecedented salary of $10,000 a week, with a bonus of $150,000. A special studio named the Lone Star was built in Hollywood and shooting commenced in March 1916.

First of the Mutuals was *The Floorwalker*, set in a department store. Memorable moments include Charlie meeting his double—a crooked manager absconding with the Store's funds—and going into a "man in the mirror" routine (a gag already used by Max Linder and later borrowed by the Marx Brothers), and a fast and funny chase up an escalator that is coming down. In true Chaplin style there is a piece of vulgarity when he serves lady customers in the shoe department.

The Fireman shows Charlie receiving his first brutal treatment from Eric Campbell (as the fire chief), but he gets his own back secretly kissing Eric's fiancée (Edna Purviance in flirtatious mood). Charlie plays checkers while Leo White's house burns down, then saves Edna who is trapped in a fire after her father tries to burn his home down for the insurance. The weakest of the series, it still works well as a laugh raiser. *The Vagabond* represented a totally new departure. At times almost a straight drama, its slapstick moments of a fight between Charlie and a German band, and Charlie rescuing Edna from the gypsies, are all over in the first reel. When it is revealed that Edna was kidnapped by the gypsies, the plot deepens while Charlie falls clumsily in love with the girl. With its moving camera work and generally restrained acting, this interesting movie was in advance of its time.

One A.M. was another experiment—a solo performance by Chaplin, as a top-hatted drunk coming home late and facing the problem of getting upstairs to bed. Although not to everyone's taste, some aficionados rate this movie very highly amongst the Chaplin *oeuvre*. Many of the versions available to collectors are shortened to one reel, missing the scenes of Charlie's struggles with a folding bed. Polishing up a routine well used at Keystone and Essanay, *The Count* has tailor's assistant Charlie masquerading as a Count. His boss Eric has the same idea, and the constant sparring of nimble Charlie and bearded Eric leads to some unbridled violent slapstick, particularly when Charlie takes sly kicks at his brutish rival on the dance floor. Like *One A.M.*, this two reeler is often released as a single reel, the slow opening sequence in the tailor's shop usually missing.

Left, two shots from One A.M. *Top right, Chaplin, Albert Austin and Eric Campbell in* **The Count.** *Below, Chaplin and Austin in the hilarious lunch-hour scene in* Behind the Screen.

A "camera look" at the end of Behind the Screen *with Edna Purviance.*

With its brilliant pantomime set pieces (the sequence with the alarm clock) and the beautifully timed by-play between Charlie and the pawnbroker's clerk (John Rand), *The Pawnshop* is one of Chaplin's finest short comedies, though Eric and Edna take relatively small parts in this classic. *Behind the Screen*, less well known than the other Mutual comedies is one of the most enjoyable. Packed with good things: Charlie's shampooing of a bear-skin rug with all the finesse of a barber, the incredibly funny lunch hour sequence (Charlie nibbles Albert Austin's meaty bone and when he's found out pretends to be a dog), and the furious pie-throwing finale when everyone gets a pie in the face except Charlie, this fast-paced comedy satirises move-making at the time. *Easy Street* is THE Chaplin classic, probably the one silent film everyone has seen. But this does not diminish its interest; apart from its set pieces—the bending of the lamp post, the crisply edited chase finale—its combination of many of Chaplin's themes and its reconstruction of the London slums of his youth make this worthy of a place in all collections. Eric Campbell is, of course, superb as the street bully. Chaplin was outstanding on roller skates, and *The Rink* gives him every chance to put this talent to comic use. Charlie's total lack of respect for Eric and the indignities piled on Eric's wife (Henry Bergman, deliciously ugly in drag) on the rink, are counterpointed by his graceful skating, and to give variety there is the funny business in the restaurant where Charlie works as a waiter. Elegantly costumed in white, Edna keeps her feminine dignity among the amorous drunks and bearded lechers in *The Cure*. Charlie, a drunk trying to dry out, runs up against gouty Eric (in another major role), and there are the usual generous number of comedy highlights (the "wrestling" match between Charlie and the masseur is particularly choice).

The Immigrant is one of the finest of all films that Chaplin made. It has social comment (the treatment of immigrants at Ellis Island), drama (the robbing of Edna's savings), comic suspense (the interplay with the coin Charlie's going to pay for his meal with), and splendid comedy (outstanding being the treatment

Top and left, trouble with an ice cream — frames from The Adventurer. *Right, a dream of marriage from the rare* The Idle Class *(once released on 9.5mm).*

meted out to customers who cannot pay their bill by Eric and his gang of waiters). Edna Purviance looks her best in this fine movie, and Eric Campbell's superb facial expressions deserve a comedy Oscar. Fast and funny, *The Adventurer* was a fitting culmination of this outstanding series of comedies. With its superbly timed chases, rarely improved upon, convict Charlie blundering in Society, and yet more chases, this is movie comedy that is hard to beat. Edna has a minor role, but once again Eric Campbell excels as the black-bearded, cowardly suitor who betrays Charlie to the police. Amidst all the fun there's the strange off beat scene where Charlie is washed up on the beach apparently drowned, played quite realistically without a comic pay-off.

Much duped, cut, titles changed, and generally tampered with, these

Next to the ABC Cinema at the Elephant and Castle, the only London pub named after a movie comedian — near Chaplin's birthplace.

comedies have suffered a lot over their sixty years of continuous exposure on the screens of the world. Print quality of new prints that are to be found is no match for the early Kodascope and Pathéscope copies, though the clear photography of William Foster and Rollie Totheroh has proved very durable in the light of constant duping. Recently Blackhawk have made especial efforts to restore the picture quality of these ever-popular comedies. In addition to tracking down the best master material available, they have remade the titles—often changed in various re-issues over the years—to make them as near as possible to Chaplin's original conception. The result of all this invaluable work is a completely new set of the Mutual comedies in Standard and Super 8 and 16mm prints. There are also sound versions on Super 8 and 16mm with music and sound effects.

UFA's Golden Age

Many major silent movies from Hollywood have constantly eluded the collector, but it has been the collector's good fortune that most of the greatest films from the legendary German UFA have been released on the narrow gauges over the years. With their enduring fascination, these amazing films have long been in demand by aficionados.

UFA (Universum Film Aktiengesellschaft), most famous of all German film companies, was formed during the First World War by the amalgamation of a number of smaller producers. Later Decla Bioskop with its production chief Erich Pommer, who had built a reputation for his ability to inspire directors, actors, and cameramen into making distinctive movies, joined forces with UFA. Such was Pommer's genius for getting the best out of his film-makers, many of them were never to repeat their outstanding work under his

Werner Krauss as Caligari.

The abduction sequence from The Cabinet of Dr. Caligari.

aegis. Some of the titles referred to below were originally produced under the Decla Bioskop banner, eventually to be released by UFA. They are, however, accepted as being a part of the UFA tradition and are treated as such here.

The Cabinet of Dr. Caligari (1919), Decla Bioskop's first major artistic triumph—psychoanalysed, dissected as a sociological phenomenon, criticised as an artistic dead-end, yet miraculously surviving as an inimitable screen experience—has long been a favourite with collectors. Werner Krauss in his top hat and shabby cloak, shuffling through the fairground, inspecting a dwarf as if he was a visitor at a zoo, feeding his somnambulist, Cesare, like a cherished infant, and alternating between mock courtesy and curt bad temper when the police inspect his caravan, brings touches of black humour to his spiky characterisation of the sinister doctor. Conrad Veidt's Cesare, looking like a monstrous spider exuded by the walls as he glides towards the sleeping girl, dominates *Caligari*'s finest moment—the abduction of the heroine, Jane (Lil Dagover), a sequence refuting the claim that *Caligari* is filmed theatre. Modern audiences will readily accept *Caligari*'s strange expressionist sets with their nerve-jangling sense of foreboding. And on subsequent viewings, for it is a film that can be seen many times without losing its power, the fascinating design and detail of its sets, and its odd mixture of horror and satire (the town hall bureaucrat sits on an absurdly high stool, the police are made to look like toy soldiers) can be fully appreciated.

Caligari, once released in an expertly abbreviated 9.5mm version of three reels (until recently available as a Standard 8 re-print), is now to be found in a full version from several sources in America, and a Super 8 condensation is released by Atlas in Germany.

In complete contrast to the macabre aura of Caligari is *Cinderella* (*Der Verlorene Schuh*), a delicate film directed with a feather-light touch by Ludwig Berger in 1923 with settings in the baroque style and some ingenious special effects. Different to the traditional fairy story—more Grimm than Perrault— this movie disproves the theory that all German silent fantasies were full of gloom. *Cinderella* was issued in a much abbreviated version on 9.5mm (until recently high spots of the trick work were included in a Standard 8 compilation, *The German Giants*).

It has been lucky for collectors that virtually all of the movies Fritz Lang directed for UFA have been available at one time or another. The earliest of his films to be found is *Der müde Tod* (*Destiny*) (1921) from Griggs Moviedrome on all the collectors' gauges. With its unforgettable figure of Death, the enormous wall with its stairway to heaven, the hall of candles—each one representing a life—and its three episodes in Bagdad, Venice and China, where the girl (Lil Dagover) tries vainly to save her lover from a predestined death, this memorable movie is in many ways superior to Lang's better known works. It even has flashes of humour amidst the spectacle and tragedy.

Like most of the UFA classics, *Siegfried* (1923)—closely following the

Siegfried: *Left, contrasts between white (symbolising good) and black (bad) that are a constant theme in the film. Right, a fine symmetrical composition – the death of Siegfried.*

ancient legend of *Die Nibelungenlied* rather than Wagner's *The Ring*—is a studio-bound production, with its forest scenes shot on the Neubabelsberg back-lot. Slow in tempo, its angular decorations with symmetrical groups of knights and ladies have the formalised appearance of stained glass windows. It is full of good things: Siegfried's battle with the fire-breathing dragon (a life-size monster operated by several men) and his encounter in the mists with the horrific Alberich, Lang's masterly way with the counterbalance of light and shade (white robed Kriemhild contrasted with the black armoured, treacherous Hagen), and the poignant death of Siegfried in the sparkling birch glade. The second part of Lang's epic, *Kriemhild's Revenge*, strikingly contrasts with the slow, stately *Siegfried*. With a theme of obsessed destruction and violence, it is far more dynamic and fast paced, but generally less interesting apart from the extraordinary playing of Rudolf Klein-Rogge as Attila.

   Siegfried and its sequel were both once available on 9.5mm in shortened, but completely satisfying, versions. Complete prints on Super 8 and 16mm are now released by Blackhawk, who have recently issued sound versions with well chosen background music.

Left, The Chronicle of Grieshuus *in which fine camerawork by Fritz Arno Wagner is a major feature. Right, Han Poelzig's set of the old castle in* Grieshuus.

Completely unlike the Langish way with a legend is *The Chronicle of Grieshuus* (1925). This important movie has apparently survived only on 9.5mm (in Britain), the BFI's 16mm copy having been duped from a Pathéscope print. One of the three films directed by the Viennese stage director Arthur von Gerlach, *Grieshuus* has warmth and the atmosphere of the real countryside instead of the introspective studio-look of Lang's chilly pageant. Impeccably photographed by Fritz Arno Wagner, its interiors glow with a mellow realism, while the location shooting on Luneberg Heath uses the swaying poplars and windswept moorland to underline the dramatic mood.

Fritz Lang's *Dr. Mabuse the Gambler* (1922) might appear to be a spin-off from *Caligari*. Like the other doctor, Lang's master criminal dabbles in the occult. He is also a Twenties' phenomenon interested in money and power, exploiting inflation. This fast moving thriller with an insidious sense of corruption and decadence, quirkily blending contemporary disaster and expressionist fantasy, owes much of its power to Rudolf Klein-Rogge whose compelling personality and penchant for disguise make him rather like a German Lon Chaney. This fascinating movie has been released on Standard 8 in America, and in a shortened Super 8 print from Atlas in Germany.

Rudolf Klein-Rogge, versatile villain at UFA.

Left, super melodrama – Gerda Maurus and Louis Ralph in The Spy.
Right, a vamp and her seducer – Lya de Putti and Warwick Ward in Vaudeville.

Although still surviving well as entertainment, *Spione* (*The Spy*) (1927), Lang's "sequel" to *Dr. Mabuse* lacks the bite of the original. Concentrating on the love affair between the agent and the woman paid to betray him, it has more in common with the romantic spy adventures of James Bond. In fact, with a train wreck engineered by the master spy (Rudolf Klein-Rogge in another composite role), a splendid chase by motor cycle and car, and the denouement in a music hall, it has influenced both the Ian Fleming yarns and Hitchcock's spy thrillers. The well abridged 9.5mm print is a collectors' "standard"; Blackhawk have a complete version on 16mm and Super 8.

Vaudeville (1925), directed by E. A. Dupont, is one of the most perfectly constructed silent films. With a minimal use of subtitles, it marked a breakthrough in the use of the camera. Calculated angles, moving camera shots, and big close ups of significant details made Karl Freund's restlessly probing camera no longer a static observer—it really put the audience in the picture. Emil Jannings suffering from his love for a worthless tart—just as he was to in *The Blue Angel*—dominates this arresting film. The almost creepy eroticism of his scenes with the sensual Lya de Putti—and the harsh reaction shots of the audience appraising the trapeze act at the Berlin Winter Gardens—give this trend-setting movie a hard-edged sexy look unusual for UFA. The shortened 9.5mm version, most highly regarded of all the Pathéscope editing jobs, is truer to the spirit of the original than the prints circulating in America in which Lya de Putti is made Janning's wife instead of his mistress, thus robbing the movie of much of its irony. An abridged print is available from Blackhawk on Standard and Super 8, and a complete 16mm version is released by Griggs Moviedrome.

Perhaps the most popular of all the UFA movies available to collectors is Fritz Lang's pioneer sci fi movie of 1926, *Metropolis*. The combination of marvellous special effects—still looking good today—and melodramatic thrills, remains strong enough to make one overlook the illogicalities and simplistic

Metropolis: *Brigitte Helm as the pure Maria and her robot counterpart.*

philosophy of Thea von Harbou's screenplay. Where would future horror movie directors from Universal's Whale to Hammer's Fisher have been without Lang's blueprint for the handling of the birth of the robot in *Metropolis*? Despite the eccentric acting of Gustav Frohlich (all swoons and tantrums), and the weak art direction in the matter of the details of life in 2000 A.D. (cars and most of the costumes are very much of the Twenties), even uninitiated audiences are caught up with its aura of excitement. It was released on 9.5mm in five reels (one of the longest movies on the gauge). Until recently it was available in a Standard 8 reproduction of the Pathéscope print, and it is currently to be found in a complete version on Super 8 and 16mm from Griggs Moviedrome.

Lya de Putti provided more of her expertise as the UFA silent vamp by playing the amoral Manon Lescaut in the movie of the same name directed by Arthur Robison in 1927, with art direction by Paul Leni (soon to go to Laemmle's Universal to make *The Cat and the Canary*). In the densely packed 9.5mm version of this elegant-looking movie, it is the early appearance of Marlene Dietrich that is best remembered.

Available on all the gauges from Griggs Moviedrome is *The Last Laugh*

Left, Lya de Putti as the wanton Manon Lescaut. *Right, Marlene Dietrich in the same film.*

(*Der Letzte Mann*) (1924), F. W. Murnau's immensely influential movie. Without titles, it uses a constantly moving camera with unflagging ingenuity to tell its simple story, scripted by the great Carl Mayer, of a doorman at a big hotel demoted to lavatory attendant. Emil Jannings excelled in the role, acting as an elderly man resplendent in Franz Josef whiskers although he was only in his late thirties.

For all its superb medieval *décor* and magical special effects, and a rumbustical performance by Jannings as Mephistopheles, Murnau's soft-centered *Faust* (1926) (available from Griggs Moviedrome on 16mm, or Milestone on Standard 8) is not as impressive as his nightmarish adaptation of Dracula, *Nosferatu* (1923). Without the UFA studio gloss, this independent production shot on location in Czechoslovakia by Fritz Arno Wagner comes over today as the best of the vampire movies. The unearthly figure of Max Schreck (a man of mystery: was he really another actor incognito?) as the rat-like vampire and the finely calculated sense of the supernatural make this another collectors' favourite. Various Standard 8 and Super 8 versions have been released, recent editions having been improved in both quality and their completeness.

Towards the end of the Twenties, UFA, backed by American money and headed again by Erich Pommer after his return from a stint with Paramount in Hollywood, adapted its distinctive style to appeal to a wider public. *The Hungarian Rhapsody* (1928), directed by Hans Schwartz, is in the new mould with the UFA studio polish combined with the open air atmosphere of the Hungarian plains. This lightweight silent "musical"—it really cries out for the talkies—is attractively played by pretty Dita Parlo, dashing Willy Fritsch, and Lil Dagover—in a new glamorous make-up. This is on 9.5mm as is the even more impressive *The Wonderful Lie* (1928), again directed by busy Hans Schwartz. A story with Anna Karenina-like echoes, with solid acting by the ever fascinating Brigitte Helm, newcomer Franz Lederer, and Warwick Ward, a British actor playing Helm's vicious husband, this movie looks forward to Hollywood's polished romantic dramas of the Thirties. From the same UFA period comes *The Prisoner's Song* (*Heimkehr*) (1928), directed by Joe May. Another triangle story, it has dependable Lars Hanson, the fine Swedish actor who appeared in several classic silent movies, losing his young wife Dita Parlo to Gustav Frohlich after the two men have escaped from a Russian prisoner of war camp. Once on 9.5mm, this worthwhile film is now to be found on 16mm from Griggs Moviedrome.

Completely different to the studio-made fantasies and legends from UFA are the "Bergfilme," the mountaineering films, a *genre* of movie unique to the German cinema of the Twenties and Thirties. Much associated with Arnold Fanck, their director, these films with their superb photography of snow and ice made an almost supernatural mystique out of mountain climbing and ski-ing. Fanck's major discovery, and favourite actress, was Leni Riefenstahl

Left, Luis Trenker, star of the German mountain films. Right, Leni Riefenstahl.

who first appeared for him in *The Sacred Mountain* (*Der Heilige Berg*) (1926), archetype of the mountain films. Their greatest film together was *The White Hell of Pitz Palu* (1929), which had Fanck handling the mountain climbing action while G. W. Pabst directed the more intimate scenes. Also featured was the First World War fighter ace Ernst Udet, who demonstrates his skill at stunt flying when he pilots his bi-plane through hazardous peaks in search for a party of missing mountaineers. Both these movies were once on 9.5mm; *White Hell* is currently to be found on Standard 8 from Milestone. It was at one time issued on 16mm.

White Hell was not made for UFA, nor were the other mountain films with Leni Riefenstahl and once released on 9.5mm: *The White Flame* (1931), a paean to skiing, and *The Blue Light* (1931), directed by Riefenstahl herself and heavy with mysticism.

Three of the finest German films made by G. W. Pabst, the most subtle of the silent directors, have been released on Standard 8 by Milestone. Although not produced by UFA, they are very much in the same tradition. *The Joyless Street* (1925), with its picture of Vienna after the First World War and memorable for Greta Garbo's appearance, is also available on Super 8 and 16mm from Griggs Moviedrome. *Secrets of a Soul* (1926) has Pabst putting his absorbing interest in psychoanalysis to work on a case history of a husband's impotence. He externalises the state of the patient's mind with all the cinematic devices at his disposal. And in *Pandora's Box* (1929), Pabst shows his uncanny ability at extracting extraordinary performances from actresses. In this, the glowingly beautiful Louise Brooks, who can now be appreciated as the major female personality of the silent screen, excels as the ultimately tragic Lulu.

Trailing behind all the UFA classics are a couple of pot-boilers to prove that the Neubabelsberg studio could crank out B movies just like any Hollywood film factory. One of these, *The Three Cuckoo Clocks* (1926), directed by Lothar Mendes, is a crisp little melodrama with the Grand Guignol pay-off of a wealthy antique collector trapped in a pool of crocodiles while thieves rob him of his treasures. And *The Little Follies Girl* (1926), directed by Hans

Schwartz, is a tedious comedy showir g there was little sense of humour around the UFA stages. Both these rarities were on 9.5mm, together with what must be the weirdest of all UFA subjects, the documentary "kultur film," *Ways to Health and Beauty* (1927), an extraordinary tract on the body beautiful and physical fitness that could be the movie version of a Nazi handbook on health.

Silence worked well for UFA. With the arrival of sound, the special flavour of the German giant's output was diminished. In tune with UFA's silent style there were however a few outstanding talkies made before Josef Goebbels took control of the German film industry and many of its finest talents emigrated to Britain and America. One or two of these are available for collectors

From Atlas in Germany comes a Super 8 condensation, and from Niles the full feature, of *M* (1931), made by Fritz Lang for Nero Film very much in the UFA manner. It has Peter Lorre in his first, and one of his greatest, screen performances as the perverted child murderer hounded down by both the police and the underworld. Emil Jannings and Marlene Dietrich are on Super 8 and 16mm (from Griggs Moviedrome) in *The Blue Angel* (1931) with the unforgettable Hollander sorg "Falling In Love Again" in its German original "Ich Bin Von Kopf Bis Fuss Auf Liebe Eingestellt". Produced by Erich Pommer for UFA, *The Blue Angel* is the sound sequel to silent expressionism. The greatest of all the movies directed by Josef von Sternberg, it constantly reminds one of *Caligari* and the other UFA silents. Conrad Veidt, one of the first stars to leave German after Hitler took control, appears in *Congress Dances* (1931). In the Atlas Super 8 condensation of one of the best of the UFA sound musicals, there is regrettably only one musical number from the original's tuneful score, sung by the Anglo-German star Lillian Harvey. Relying on a knowledge of German for its full enjoyment, this is an interesting souvenir of a movie rarely shown these days.

Gags and Gadgets—
The Films of Snub Pollard

Comedy—most durable of silent film *genres*—was not just Chaplin, Keaton, Lloyd, and Langdon. There were the second string comedians too; comics who flickered across the screen for their fleeting hours of popularity, still affectionately remembered for the fun they provided. Without the ambition or the distinctive personality to make the big time, every now and then these skilled clowns would make a comedy well out of the rut of the routine shorts cranked out by the fun factories. Like Snub Pollard, for example.

Snub Pollard, born in Australia, began his show business career as a juvenile in musical comedy and like so many small time players was lured to Hollywood. He appeared in bit parts, striking lucky when he was teamed with Harold Lloyd in the Lonesome Luke comedies for Hal Roach in 1915. During these knockabout romps he hit on his comedy trade-mark—a large droopy moustache—said to have been invented when he put on a "Kaiser" moustache upside-down.

Dozens of short comedies were made for the Luke series, but few have survived. Even fewer have appeared on the collectors' gauges, and perhaps the best known is *Luke's Movie Muddle* (1917) sometimes called *Director of the Cinema*, which has appeared on all the gauges. In this Harold is manager, usher, and cashier of a down-town movie house, Snub is the projectionist getting tangled up with the film. In common with most of these early Hal Roach comedies the humour is crude and unsubtle, Luke a far from likeable character. These were the rough and ready days of movie production; a camera was set up and situations worked out off the cuff. When Harold ditched the Luke characterisation—which was little more than the Chaplin screen *persona* of the time in reverse—and took on his celebrated horn-rimmed glasses, the quality of his comedy improved considerably. In such pleasant comedies as *Spring Fever* and *Just Neighbours*, Harold and Snub work admirably as a team in situations shot against the parks and streets of the Hollywood area. Eventually, the team broke up and Snub Pollard was given his own series by Hal Roach. He made over one hundred single reel comedies for Roach's laughter machine, many of which are lost. Fortunately for collectors some of the best items are still to be found.

Ingenious gags and gadgetry form a large part of these clever comedies, for

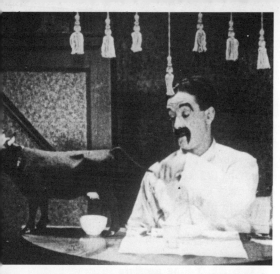

Snub Pollard in the classic
It's a Gift. *Top, self-service breakfast in bed. Centre, "garbage" without the "b" equals garage. Below, the magnet car.*

Snub, although an amusing comic, did not have the strong screen presence of the comedy "greats." He needed a good comedy situation for success, and was fortunate in having the inventive comedy creator Charley Chase as his director—at this time Charley had taken a break from appearing on the screen to work on the other side of the camera under his real name of Charles Parrott. One of the best is *Sold at Auction* (1923), a wild and weird affair with Snub mistakenly selling up the Sheriff's home and then having to recover all the goods. It finishes with Snub speeding along busy streets on a grand piano using the pedals as controls until a speed cop catches up with him. This is on 9.5mm as is *Years to Come* (9.5mm title: *A Day Will Come*) which reverses the roles of man and wife. Snub does the housework while his bossy masculine wife goes to the office—a situation well milked for laughs. In this prophetic look forward to Women's Lib, ugly Hal Roach heavy Noah Young appears in drag as an unlikely maid, and in one scene Snub is caught for a moment laughing at Young (a glimpse that escaped the Roach editor's scissors!). There's more eccentric fun in *365 Days* (9.5mm title: *Fortune Hunters*) with Snub living in a bungalow suspended from a balloon to qualify for a legacy. His baby puts a dollar in the gas meter and the balloon floats skywards, eventually landing on the railroad in front of an oncoming train. In *The Courtship of Miles Sandwich* (1923), a spoof of a Charles Ray vehicle, Snub appears in a hilariously anachronistic look at the arrival of the Pilgrim Fathers (on Super 8 from Blackhawk).

Inventive ideas, these, but none matched the classic *It's a Gift* (1923) directed by Ralph Cedar, released on 9.5mm in 1928 and now to be obtained from Blackhawk on Super 8. Snub is an inventor, introduced in a bed surrounded by ropes manipulating an incredible array of Heath Robinson (or, if you prefer, Rube Goldberg) style gadgets that actually work. He breakfasts in bed with the aid of these labour saving devices, nonchalantly tugging the ropes to bring them into action. Funny though these moments are, they only raise chuckles. But a surprise payoff brings a belly laugh: after breakfast Snub folds his bed into the wall revealing a fire-place—with a fire burning cheerfully in the grate!

Summoned to demonstrate his gasoline substitute, Snub sets forth in his tiny car propelled by a large magnet which is attracted by a passing car. He gets along well until his magnet pulls the body from the chassis of a model T Ford to the annoyance of the courting couple in it. Hal Roach's property department kept a whole fleet of dissectible model T's for gags like this.

Then comes a perfect piece of gag construction, typical of silent comedy at its best. Snub passes a cop sitting on top of a garbage can while flirting with a nursemaid. The magnet whisks away the garbage can: the cop tumbles into the gutter (the audience chuckles). In a long shot, the cop gives chase, while a tracking shot has Snub shaking the garbage can from the magnet—it falls in the road. Again in long shot the cop stumbles over the garbage can (the audience laughs). Back to Snub passing over a man-hole—the magnet whisks off the cover. The cop gets to his feet and continues the chase. Cut to a tracking shot of

Snub looking back—and in extreme long shot the cop disappearing down the open man-hole (the audience roars!).

Less skilled comedies would extract one laugh from the cop and garbage can situation, but here slickly timed editing—each shot makes its point and no more—and an inventive triple-tiered gag bring a crescendo of laughter. At the demonstration, Snub doles out his wonder fuel—"one drop for automobiles, two for flivvers" says the title. Shot at one frame per second the cars career about madly, meeting together in a spectacular collison and explosion—a sequence, incidentally, that has been much used in TV compilations on comedy and motoring. Snub gets the last laugh after the disaster; when chased off by a motorcycle cop his magnet car sprouts wings—and takes off into the sky for a neat iris out. . . .

It was difficult for Pollard to equal this one reel gem. In 1924, he recreated his crazy inventor character in *The Big Idea* (on Super 8 from Blackhawk) demonstrating his incredible "Patent Pavement Polisher"—a street cleaning vacuum cleaner (oddly enough an idea that has actually appeared in more recent times). There is some clever business when Snub consults a patent attorney, who rapidly changes his bedroom into an efficient looking office (a direct imitation of Pollard's bedroom in *It's a Gift*) and some mild satire at the expense of local government big-wigs: they play cat's cradle instead of watching his demonstration. But like other sequels, this comedy fails to match the non-stop gagging of the original.

Other Pollard comedies made while he was under contract to Hal Roach that are available on Standard and Super 8 from Blackhawk include *Before the Public* (1923), *The Dumb Bell* (1922), and *In the Grease* (1925). In the Roach Pollard shorts, Snub's supporting cast includes pretty, brown-eyed Marie Mosquini as his wife or girl-friend and brutish Noah Young as the heavy, occasionally aided and abetted by Laurel and Hardy's nemesis Jimmy Finlayson giving his usual line in pop-eyed villainy. Extracts from some fine Roach Pollards are included in *Days of Thrills and Laughter* (1961), Robert Youngson's superb feature length evocation of the fun and excitement of cinema going in the silent days, available on Super 8 sound from Powell Films.

After his long association with Hal Roach, Snub formed his own company in 1926. Like other unwise comedians he was persuaded that he could do better on his own with greater control over his work. These movies were distributed by Weiss Brothers Artcraft on the independent market. The results were poor; without the expertise of the Roach organisation, Pollard was just a run-of-the-mill funny man. They were the last movies Pollard was to star in, and he was to lose all his money in their production. Under changes titles, shortened versions of one or two of these comedies have been released on Super 8 by Mountain Films, part of a block of Chuckleheads shorts made up for TV by the successors of Weiss Brothers.

In the thirties Snub Pollard was to provide the obligatory comic relief that was a tradition in B Westerns, in particular in the batch of movies Tex Ritter made for Monogram, where Pollard was the doleful Pee Wee. Occasionally he landed bit parts in more prestigious movies, notably Chaplin's *Limelight* (1952) as a wizened street musician. But Snub Pollard (1886–1962) is best remembered for *It's a Gift*, a true classic of the one reel comedy form.

The Great Mosjoukine

Unique—even in an era full of larger than life personalities—Russian actor Ivan Mosjoukine had his hour of fame in the Twenties, yet he is hardly remembered today. A refugee from the Revolution, he was the star of a talented group of Russian film-makers who emigrated to Paris in 1920. With him was his wife, Nathalie Lissenko, who partnered him in many of his films, and his favourite director Alexander Volkov. In the old Montreuil studio built by Georges Méliès, these Russians, under the name of Albatros with Alexander Kamenka as their producer, started work on some distinctive films combining their novel ideas with the latest French experiments. The 9.5mm collector is lucky; several of Mosjoukine's most celebrated movies were released on this gauge. Although often savagely cut, even the short versions recapture his compelling personality and offbeat sense of humour. The earliest, and needless to say, rarest Mosjoukine subject is *L'Enfant du Carnival* (1921), which has him as a rich playboy giving shelter to an abandoned child, an experience that brings new meaning to his life. It was only issued in France in a mere 180 ft.

Kean (1923) is a fascinating fragment. It tells of the chequered life of the unbalanced Eighteenth Century English actor, allowing Mosjoukine to re-enact many of Kean's famous roles as well as scenes of his turbulent off-stage life. One high spirited sequence has Kean frightening away some creditors by getting his manager to don a tiger skin rug. Kean leaves his home disguised as a sailor—with his manager in drag as an old woman. As they hurry away, the "old woman's" skirt falls, revealing trousers—in a scene which is handled with all the flair of a Keystone comedy. Later there is a brief flash of the celebrated rapidly-cut sequence in which Kean dances the horn-pipe with reckless abandon. Kean's death is beautifully portrayed—intercut with a wind-swept birch tree and a melancholy howling dog. Symbolic curtains fall across the scene; the play of Kean's life is ended. Superb settings and photography—by J. L. Mundviller—make this single reel version a precious reminder of Mosjoukine's work. Sufficient remains for the appreciation of his daring blend of low comedy and high drama, ably directed by the inventive Volkov.

In the comedy-drama *Passing Shadows* (1924), the setting is again England, Mosjoukine plays a country lad brought up as a trusting child of nature by his father, a cranky professor of ethics. The young man comes into a legacy, going alone to Paris to collect it, where he is soon the prey of gold-diggers. After an affair with a mysterious countess (Nathalie Lissenko), he is found and taken back to his country home by his distracted wife and father. Once again there are

Kean: *the actor and his manager in disguise.*

Passing Shadows: *Mosjoukine and Natalie Lissenko.*

Michael Strogoff: *courier of the Czar.*

Mosjoukine in The Lion of the Moguls.

touches of broad humour: a strait-laced country vicar collapses when he sees Mosjoukine and his wife—wearing bathing suits—gallop by on horseback; in a Parisian restaurant scene Mosjoukine struggles with a pepper-pot, his violent sneezes blowing a pancake clean off his plate; and there is a burlesque of serial-style melodramatics when he is kidnapped from the countess's villa. The tone switches to drama when he is stabbed by the thugs. Tragedy reappears at the film's end, when the broken-hearted countess walks to the sea—and her death. In a poignant final shot, her black shawl, caught in the rocks, is gently ruffled by the sea breeze.

Between these films Mosjoukine wrote, directed, and starred in *Le Brasier Ardent* (1923). Not available to collectors, this rarely seen comedy-fantasy tells of a woman's nightmare in which Mosjoukine appears in many guises. Later she meets him in real life as a detective called to solve a robbery at her home. She falls in love with him, and their adventures together parallel the incidents in her dream. Imaginatively using rapid cutting, projected negative, stop motion, and speeded action, this engaging film is Mosjoukine's masterpiece, proving him one of the silent cinema's most original creators. What makes this movie so enjoyable is that the effects are all done for fun, without the pretentiousness of most *avant-garde* experiments. It is just the kind of film any collector of silent movies would love to own.

Coming after such full-blooded films, *The Lion of the Moguls* (1924) is a disappointment. It has a feeble plot—for which Mosjoukine was responsible. A Tibetan prince flees from a cruel Khan; on the ship to France he is "discovered" by a film company, becoming a star; he finds his long-lost sister; is nearly murdered; and finally returns in triumph to Tibet. Though there are typical Mosjoukine touches in the early scenes, such as his moments as the tempestuous lover battling with the Khan's guards, the rest of the film is static and unexciting, only occasionally enlivened by some fascinating shots of the film company at work, and a few unusual camera effects (again by Mundviller). A dull film to have come from such a talented director as Jean Epstein.

The experimental days were over and Mosjoukine left Albatros. He triumphed in L'Herbier's *Le Feu Matthias Pascal* (not available to collectors), nearly appeared as Napoleon for Abel Gance, but starred instead in *Michael Strogoff* (1926), directed by another Russian emigré director V. Tourjansky. This outstanding movie is based on a Jules Verne story of a courier carrying secret papers from the Czar to the Governor of a province threatened by hostile Tarter rebels. Authentic locales (it was shot on location in Lithuania), some inventive montage (at the start of the film striking camera angles of dancing couples at a court ball, similar to some of Busby Berkeley's favourite camera positions, are intercut with shots of charging Tartar hordes), and a vigorous sword fight finale make this a good adventure film that has worn its years lightly. The well edited three reel 9.5mm version is a prized collectors' piece.

Michael Strogoff brought Mosjoukine world fame. He was enticed to Hollywood by Universal to appear in *Surrender* (1927), starring as a Cossack cavalry officer—and prince!—who leads a detachment of horsemen into a village on the Austro–Hungarian borders in the First World War. While out riding he meets the beautiful daughter of the leader of the Jewish community, falling in love with her. When she refuses his advances, he threatens to kill all the people in the village. Great pressure is put on the girl to meet the Cossack's demand by the frightened villagers, but for a long time she stubbornly holds out, until she finally succumbs to the ruthless charm of the suave aristocrat. An unusual movie from Hollywood, *Surrender* has much of the flavour of one of Mosjoukine's continental films with its creative camerawork, by Gilbert Warrenton, and detailed direction by British-born Edward Sloman. It was released in its full length from the Wallace Heaton library on 16mm. In recent times a satisfactory Standard 8 print has been available of this unusual subject.

Surrender was to be Mosjoukine's only American film. It was not a box-office hit. American moviegoers likened Mosjoukine to comic Larry Semon so the Russian star returned to Europe to appear in the Franco–German spectacular *Casanova* (1927), directed by his original collaborator Alexander Volkov, a lavish comedy ideally suited to Mosjoukine's talents. Remarkable for a silent movie, it featured some nude scenes, a few moments of which have survived in the five reel 9.5mm version. Pathéscope went to town with this release, using different colour tinted stock to reproduce the effects of the original cinema prints. Mosjoukine made a few other silent movies, which never seem to see the light of a projector these days—even if they still exist—and then his career went into decline largely because his heavy Russian accent was not acceptable in talkies. He took to drink, supporting himself as a dance partner in a cabaret, and died in 1939 in Paris at the age of 50. It is ironic that his talent is probably only celebrated today because a few of his movies happened to get released on 9.5mm.

Lon Chaney and The Unholy Three

There can be little doubt that Lon Chaney (1883–1930) was one of the most remarkable performers of the silent era, one of the few actors who were able to transcend the limitations of the medium to give performances that were both moving and powerful. And these roles have proved durable on the screen today. Not a great many of his films have survived and the number available for collectors is few. There is the melodrama *The Trap* (1922) to be found on Standard 8. Chaney is a simple-minded French Canadian befriending the small son of his rival who is in jail. When the man who enticed his *fiancée* away many years before is finally released, Chaney builds a trap containing a hungry wolf in the hopes of killing his hated rival. But the boy gets caught instead. In this old time story of revenge—the sub-titles are classics of flowery prose—Chaney's strong pantomime still shines through. *The Hunchback of Notre Dame* is a collectors' standard, as is his pioneer horror film *The Phantom of the Opera* (1925). It is a shrewd blend of spectacle (the Paris Opera and the Phantom's sub-terranean lair), serial style melodramatics (the hero trapped in a torture chamber and battling with rising flood waters), and Beauty and the Beast fantasy (the heroine in the clutches of the ghastly Phantom). In its sensational scenes (the massive chandelier crashing down into the stalls of the Opera, the unmasking of the Phantom by the inquisitive heroine to reveal his hideous features, the Phantom swimming under the water of an underground lake to strike the unwary intruders) the action is kept merrily on the boil.

As Erik the Phantom, Chaney dominates the film. His vigorous pantomime hits the right note in this large scale piece of hokum; only occasionally does his acting tip into ham. In the exciting climax, he has captured the girl (beautiful Mary Philbin), offering her the grim choice of either blowing the Opera sky high or giving herself to him and saving her *fiancé*. Suspense is built up by cross-cutting her *fiancé* struggling in the flooded torture chamber with vast crowds of rescuers in torchlight procession marching down massive flights of steps to round up the Phantom.

Although the photographic quality of Standard and Super 8 versions of this popular movie varies considerably, it is possible to get quite acceptable prints. It is also possible to find the celebrated Bal Masque sequence, originally shot in an early two-colour process, presumably Technicolor, as a Super 8 colour print reproducing the red cloak and skull mask of the Phantom most effectively. This short sequence can be spliced into the feature to make it an even more spectacular collectors' piece.

Lon Chaney, above in The Hunchback of Notre Dame, *below in* The Phantom of the Opera.

What is not well known is that three of Lon Chaney's major movies for MGM, all directed by Tod Browning, were issued by Pathé Baby in France on 9.5mm: *The Road to Mandalay* (1926), *The Unknown* (1927), and *The Unholy Three* (1925). Perhaps *The Road to Mandalay* is the least impressive, a tepid affair with little action, though Lon Chaney excels as the half-blind evil brother. In many ways *The Unknown* is the most powerful of the three. Lon Chaney is a knife thrower in a Madrid circus whose arms are bound to his sides hiding the two thumbs he has on each hand which would identify him as a wanted murderer. He throws his knives with his feet! Finding that the girl he loves (an early major role for Joan Crawford) cannot bear to be touched, he decides to have his arms amputated to please her. Unfortunately, while he is away having this operation, she overcomes her fear and falls for the circus strong-man. Chaney becomes completely unhinged and attempts a macabre revenge so that his rival's arms are nearly torn off by two horses galloping in opposite directions. Infected by a disturbingly evil atmosphere, this story of perverse relationships and dismemberment is rather sick even by modern standards.

The Unholy Three is the best of this trio because it hits just the right target with its skilful combination of the bizarre, suspense and black comedy. At a fairground, Hercules, a strong man, Echo, a ventriloquist, and Tweedledee, a midget, are all sideshows acts. Echo, obviously crooked, has a racket as a sideline; his girl-friend Rose mingles with the audience and picks pockets while they are enjoying the acts. When Tweedledee appears, a couple of "flappers" tease him about his size, and things take an ugly turn when he kicks a little boy who is laughing at him in the face. The scene breaks up in confusion when the crowd react angrily to the vicious midget. Then the police arrive . . .

Shadows on the wall introduce Echo, conspiratorially explaining to Hercules and Tweedledee how he's got an idea that will make them a fortune. Later a pet store opens, owned by Mrs. O'Grady—apparently a dear old lady— with Hercules, Tweedledee and Rose in the background. The manager of the shop is the timid Hector, keen on Rose. Mrs. O'Grady is, of course, Echo in drag.

Echo's new racket concerns the parrots his shop has for sale. The birds speak beautifully in the shop (somewhat crudely, superimposed cartoon caption "balloons" make this point) but when the wealthy customers get the parrots home they fail to talk. If they complain, Mrs. O'Grady obligingly calls round to convince them that the birds do really talk (don't forget that Echo is a ventriloquist) taking her baby "grandson" with her. When wealthy Mr. Arlington complains, Mrs. O'Grady obliges as usual, and "she" and the "baby" note the valuable string of rubies in the house.

The whole of the conviction of this bizarre tale depends on the convincing portrayals of Echo/Mrs. O'Grady and Tweedledee/baby. Lon Chaney is excellent as the larcenous old lady, cleverly investing the apparently benign old soul with a sinister streak. But like animals and children on the screen,

Lon Chaney as Mrs. O'Grady in The Unholy Three.

Harry Earles' midget/baby steals the show. He is amazing as the baby, totally convincing, lying in the pram in his woolly suit and bootees, with his tiny hands grasping the jewels. Although small in size, he is sinister, too. In a touch of black humour, he struts about in a fur collared overcoat and bowler hat, chewing a cigar like a miniature gangster when he's out of his baby clothes.

The next day Arlington is found murdered. Because they have been seen near the Arlington home not long before the killing, a police inspector calls on Mrs. O'Grady and her "baby." Echo hurriedly dons his wig when he realises the inspector is about to call, yanks the cigar from Tweedledee's mouth and stuffs it into the mouth of the surprised Hercules. The inspector (wryly played by Matthew Betz, whose usual forte was villains) picks up the "baby's" toy elephant and idly nods its head (previously Tweedledee has hidden the stolen rubies in the toy), while he questions the Unholy Three.

With almost comic suspense, cross-cutting the inspector's playing with the elephant and the increasingly agitated Echo and Hercules, it looks as though the hidden jewels have been discovered when the policeman realises the toy rattles. In panic, Hercules accuses the policeman of teasing the baby, snatches the elephant away from the inspector and gives it back to Tweedledee who coolly gets out a sweet to eat! This well sustained sequence is the best in the film, and it is interesting to find there is a similar sequence with some jewels hidden in a toy in Browning's fantasy thriller of 1935, *The Devil Doll.* Before long, Hector is arrested for the murder and taken to police headquarters for questioning. As things are getting hot around the pet store, Hercules, Tweedledee and Rose all leave for a hideout in the country. Echo also sends along with them a large gorilla from the pet store and as he is unrecognisable to the suspicious police when dressed as a man he stays behind to keep an eye on events. The action with the gorilla—a formidable beast—is handled most ingeniously. Obviously, it would be impossible to train a real gorilla as a screen performer, a situation that is usually overcome by having an actor in a gorilla skin, looking ridiculously unconvincing. Browning uses a large circus ape and to increase its apparent size the scenes in which it appears have scaled-down sets. For example, when the beast gets into the crooks' caravan, a small foreground figure of Echo frames the action (in fact, it looks as though the diminutive back of Harry Earles stands in for Chaney's burly frame!). To enhance the illusion of a large lumbering ape, the scenes with the animal are all shot in slow motion. The climax of this fantastic tale comes with the trial of Hector and the quarrelling of Hercules, Tweedledee and Rose regarding the stolen jewels. While the noose tightens round Hector, Hercules, at the hide-out, tries to persuade Rose to run away with him, taking the jewels with them. Furious, little Tweedledee lets the ape loose. Out of camera range it attacks and kills the strong man. Rose runs screaming from the cabin to find the police have arrived—they are still looking for the missing witnesses. Back at the court, Echo becomes more and more disturbed when he realises Hector will hang—finally blurting out the truth in a court-room confession.

Tod Browning (1882–1962) ran away from school to join a circus and had become a vaudeville comic by the time he joined Biograph studios as an actor. He played in and was an assistant director to D. W. Griffith on *Intolerance*. Then from 1918 to 1923 he left acting and became a director of routine subjects for Universal. He really got into his stride at MGM in 1925 and after, where he directed the extraordinary series of films that made his name as a specialist in the grotesque and macabre with Chaney—an old Universal colleague—as his star. In the early sound era, he gained further fame with *Dracula* (surely his most famous film), the much banned *Freaks*, and the ingenious *Devil Doll*. If the "auteur" theory has any validity at all, Browning is as good an example of an auteur as any Hollywood director. His penchant for bizarre—sometimes perversely morbid—subjects is unprecedented in screen history; he was obviously a director with an obsession. And it is amazing that he was able to give full reign to his unique imagination under the super efficient producership of Irving Thalberg, originally at Universal, who invited him to join the newly formed MGM. Despite their morbid subject matter, Browning has little violence in his films, preferring the use of suggestion. So in *The Unholy Three* we do not see the gorilla attack Hercules. And in *Dracula* we never see the final dissolution of the vampire; it takes place off screen. Not a director to use cinematic fireworks, Browning was painstaking in extracting the maximum effect from the strange subjects and characters that he made, uniquely, his own.

Britain's Silent Hollywood

In the early Twenties British film production was at its lowest ebb; the big studios of Hollywood, geared to mass production, completely dominated with their vast output. The situation became so bad that in 1927 even the *laissez-faire* Government took action to save British production from extinction by introducing the famous Quota Act which made it obligatory for all British cinemas to show a proportion of British films. The green light had been given for large scale production.

Foremost among the new production companies set up as a result of the Quota Act was British International Pictures, the brainchild of John Maxwell, a Scottish solicitor who already owned a chain of cinemas and a distribution organisation. Ambitious in concept, the idea behind BIP was to produce films of international appeal as well as for the home market. The studios, built at Elstree in 1927, were to be as good as any in the world, a centre where top

The Boreham Wood studio of British International Pictures, circa 1931.

talents could make outstanding films. The 28-years-old Alfred Hitchcock—already acclaimed as Britain's best director after his strong way with a thriller, *The Lodger*, in 1926—was contracted to make movies on British themes, reckoned to do well throughout the Empire as well as on the home market. At an unprecedented salary of £10,000 a year, he started work at Elstree on an original screenplay he wrote himself, *The Ring*. And who better to direct sophisticated movies likely to appeal to America and Europe than E. A. Dupont, hot from his success with the brilliant *Vaudeville*, one of the most influential German silents?

Hitchcock had a first-rate British cinematographer, Jack Cox, behind the camera on his films, and German cameramen such as Theodor Sparkuhl and Werner Brandes as well as the German set designer Alfred Junge were employed to bring new style and opulence to BIP's output. With more money being spent on their production than had been devoted to earlier films, the penny-pinching look that had become the trade-mark of British studios disappeared.

Thus, in the last couple of years of the silent era, Elstree produced the best British films ever made up to then; but although most of the BIP films are, fortunately, preserved at the National Film Archive (and rarely, if ever, shown), they might have been completely overlooked by silent enthusiasts had it not been for 9.5mm. The best of BIP's silent output released on 9.5mm provides an admirable cross-section of the time when some of the major talents of the silent screen converged on Elstree to make it Britain's mini-Hollywood.

Hitchcock's first BIP film, *The Ring*, was not a suspense thriller, but in keeping with the "film stories about Britain" policy, a realistic, exciting tale about a boxer who works his way from a fairground booth to a championship bout at the Albert Hall and nearly loses his wife in the process. Spiced by characteristic Hitchcock touches, it showed that British films could have as much flair as any.

E. A. Dupont's first BIP film was *Moulin Rouge*, set against the exotic background of the famous Parisian music hall. A novelettish triangle story of a young man who falls for his girl-friend's glamorous mother, it was lavishly produced and stylishly photographed, but was little more than a re-make of the

Monty Banks, star comedian at B.I.P., in Weekend Wives.

successful *Vaudeville*—a case of observing the principle of following up a box-office hit with a sequel. Hitchcock's next two movies failed to live up to the promise of *The Ring*. He had gone on record as rating *Champagne*, a weak comedy whose sole appeal is breezy Betty Balfour, as his worst film, and *The Manxman* is basically soap opera stylishly served up. These three Hitchcock films were all cut to two reel versions on 9.5mm. They have been reprinted on 16mm in America, released as *The Alfred Hitchcock Trilogy*.

Some unusual acting talents were also attracted to Elstree. The bouncy little Italian comedian, Monty Banks, who went to Hollywood and made some fine comedies—notably *Play Safe* (on 8mm), a *tour de force* of dangerous stunting when Monty gets caught on a runaway train—became BIP's star comic. In *Adam's Apple* (*Monty's Honeymoon* on 9.5mm) he does some hair-raising antics dangling by his braces from the top window of a tall London hotel, but his best Elstree comedy was *Weekend Wives*. This was a sophisticated farce with Monty as a Parisian man about town spending a weekend at Deauville with the wife of a lawyer friend who also turns up with a fast lady client. Then her husband arrives, gunning for her boy friend. In a riot of misunderstanding Monty thinks the murderous husband is out to get him! Excellently directed by Harry Lachman, it artfully blends Monty's clever slapstick with sexy situations.

The fascinating Chinese actress Anna May Wong came from Hollywood to star in Dupont's best film for BIP, *Piccadilly*. With its German director, cameraman and set designer, and its completely studio-bound atmosphere, it could almost have come from UFA. Written specially for the screen by Arnold Bennett, it is about the murder of a Chinese dancer who replaces the temperamental mistress of a nightclub owner (Jameson Thomas). Charles Laughton has a memorable cameo role as a drunken diner who creates a scene over a dirty plate and is the cause of Thomas's visit to the kitchens where he discovers the sinuous Chinese dish-washer dancing to amuse the other staff. Once again Dupont was working in his familiar territory of a triangle situation set against a show-biz background. He excelled himself with scintillating lighting effects when Anna May Wong makes her debut in a voluptuous Balinese dance. Ingeniously, he picked up the theme of sparkling shafts of light with a big close-

Anna May Wong as the exotic oriental dancer in Piccadilly.

Anna May Wong and Jameson Thomas in Piccadilly.

up of the crystal knob turning on the door of Thomas' mistress's flat. There were eye-catching effects, too, in the scenes of the nightclub kitchen and the strange oriental shop where Thomas buys Anna May Wong's bizarre costume. The full 8 reel version of *Piccadilly* can be obtained on Standard 8 from Milestone.

Not all the BIP films were dominated by the fireworks of the Germans and Hitchcock's ingenious touches. There was the conventional patriotic movie *Tommy Atkins*, with a spectacular battle as its climax photographed on location in Egypt by Claude Friese Greene, the talented cinematographer son of the inventor who claimed to be the originator of motion pictures. Betty Balfour starred in *The Vagabond Queen*, photographed by the master cameraman Charles Rosher—a sparkling comedy notable for its witty subtitles which are an entertainment in themselves. It is based on *The Prisoner of Zenda*, cheeky Cockney Betty standing in for a Ruritanian queen. The ever bright Betty partnered Charlie Chaplin's brother Syd in an adaptation of a stage farce *A Little Bit of Fluff*. Its high spot is a wildly slapstick restaurant scene, completely uncharacteristic of the BIP style. Elstree was also enterprising in turning an item in the news, the record-breaking locomotive The Flying Scotsman, into topical entertainment. *The Flying Scotsman* offered serial style thrills when Pauline Johnson chambers along the coaches of the crack express to save it from

Tommy Atkins: *tales from the Empire.*

Ray Milland in his first starring role in The Flying Scotsman.

The perils of Pauline Johnson in The Flying Scotsman.

Lars Hanson in The Informer, *at right with Lya de Putti and Carl Harbord.*

destruction. This splendid thriller was shot on the genuine locations without studio special effects to mar the realism; an outrigger camera mount was built for photographing the action as the train thundered along the tracks.

One of the greatest German directors was Dr. Arthur Robison, a doctor of medicine who turned to the movies. His titleless *Warning Shadows* is one of the masterpieces of the expressionistic style, so it is only to be expected that his version of *The Informer* is something special. In fact, it is the most distinguished silent film produced by BIP. With the Hungarian Lya de Putti and the Swedish Lars Hanson curiously but effectively cast in the leading roles, this grim story of the troubles in Ireland in the early Twenties (tragically still topical today) has rare style and atmosphere. Although its studio-built streets have little sense of the Irish scene, the finely composed and strikingly lit shots, edited with superb precision, give it all the power of the taut crime thrillers that were to appear from Hollywood in the following decade. It is in all ways superior to John Ford's embarrassingly pretentious Oscar-winning version of the same story. A Standard 8 reprint from a 9.5mm copy is currently available from Milestone Movies.

The Informer was caught up in the arrival of sound. It was a new headache for British producers which could not be ignored, and some of the sequences were re-shot with dialogue before its release. But Elstree's first major talkie was to be significant in British film history. It was *Blackmail*, a crime thriller directed by Alfred Hitchcock. After the poor run of subjects forced on him by the studio heads, Hitchcock suggested a story more in his line, a thriller written for the stage by Charles Bennett. He and the author adapted the plot as a silent film, but after shooting was completed it became clear that the days of silence were numbered, so the drastic decision was taken to salvage the scenes not needing synchronised sound and to re-shoot the remainder as a talkie. Unlike many "all sound and talking" efforts from the infancy of sound, *Blackmail* is not short on exciting action sequences. There is a splendid chase through London streets featuring the Flying Squad, and the blackmailer is finally cornered in the British Museum, a setting achieved with some impressive special effects (an area in which Hitchcock has sometimes revealed a blind spot).

The 9.5mm edition is an abbreviation of the silent version prepared at the time for cinemas without sound equipment and most of the key scenes with Hitchcock's visual touches survive intact. There is no doubt that this was the director's first masterpiece. With its themes of guilty conscience and violence set against familiar London backgrounds, it was a pointer to many later successes. Echoes of it re-appear in Hitchcock's recent film *Frenzy*, with its accent on murder set in the London scene. Unhappily, the imaginatively constructed *Blackmail*, an auspicious start for sound movies in Britain, did not help Elstree realise its ambitions to become a second Hollywood, and subsequent films for BIP—apart from some more experiments with subjective sound in the thriller, *Murder*—lacked *Blackmail*'s creative fire. And Dupont's final fling with the

Blackmail. *Top left, a triangle of suspicion – John Longden, Annie Ondra and Donald Calthrop. Top right, Annie Ondra. Bottom left, Donald Calthrop. Bottom right, the chase through the British Museum.*

Monty Banks directing Chili Bouchier.

first multi-lingual talkie, *Atlantic*, based on the sinking of the Titanic, was ruined by some grotesquely slow-paced dialogue.

The Germans returned home without having influenced British film-making, Monty Banks made a new career as a director of comedy stars such as George Formby, and Anna May Wong returned to Hollywood. Then BIP turned away from "big pictures" to settle in a rut of domestic comedies, lightweight dramas, and musicals featuring radio stars until, under a new name, there was a renaissance when more important movies were produced at Elstree after the war.

Part Six

16mm Sound Collecting

For some dedicated movie collectors, 16mm sound is the collecting medium par excellence. And in many ways they are right, for 16mm offers print quality and a choice of subjects rivalling 35mm. As most colleges and schools have 16mm sound projectors, it is also a popular format with teachers of film appreciation who need to have prints of classic films in constant use for study purposes. At the same time it is the most controversial of the gauges for collectors when it comes to questions of copyright and piracy.

Although most aspects of movie collecting which have been discussed in detail in this volume are common to all the gauges—and apply equally to 16mm sound—there are certain features of the handling and sources of this gauge which are special. Because of this, it is important that the would-be collector of "the amateur gauge that turned professional" should be aware of its snags and pitfalls as well as its advantages. So this chapter describes the background of 16mm sound, the present situation with regard to copyright and illicit duping, and covers some of the legally available titles of especial interest for collectors.

A 16mm sound projector was designed by R. C. May of RCA in 1930 (in fact, so good was the design it remained unsurpassed for the next decade), and films for the machine soon became available. Initially 16mm sound was much orientated to education in common with the early days of 9.5mm and 16mm silent movies. And before the Second World War it only made modest progress as a home entertainer. After all, it was very cheap to go to the movies in the Thirties and enterprising theatres provided lavish programmes with added attractions like live shows and giveaways, while 16mm was expensive, beyond the reach of most people. However, there were excellent 16mm projectors manufactured by Bell and Howell, Ampro and Victor, usually based around the design of their silent machines.

The major movie companies did not take 16mm sound particularly seriously during this period (any more than they had concerned themselves with 9.5mm or 16mm) so that the majority of films for the projector owner were virtually all from independents, though Bell and Howell did operate a comprehensive library with a good selection of titles produced by Universal.

In Britain, one company that did show confidence in 16mm sound was the Gaumont British Picture Corporation, a movie empire covering production and exhibition, which manufactured professional sound equipment through their British Acoustic division. The result was the introduction of a range of 16mm sound projectors (the Gebescopes) which became the best known of all the

British made machines. To back up the projectors, G.B. were able to release an impressive range of movies from their own theatrical output, and many important British sound movies of the Thirties were issued on the new gauge. (Interestingly, some of the same titles are now available legally on 16mm in the United States and are referred to at the end of this chapter.)

Came the war and 16mm sound got a shot in the arm at just the right moment in its development. With its portable, lightweight projectors and less bulky film, it rapidly became the prime source of entertainment for troops on active service and a major factor in the training of recruits for both the forces and the industry of the Allies and the Axis. With this important extension to the 35mm theatrical distribution of their features, major movie companies began to have printed on 16mm sound all their productions around about the time of their release to the theatres. Along with this wider use of 16mm came technical improvements. It had been apparent that many early 16mm prints had poor sound, and techniques—like the re-recording of sound tracks to suit the smaller format—began to be adopted for making 16mm sound copies.

16mm had now become a practical second best to 35mm. The narrower gauge was a professional entertainment medium with mobile movie shows on 16mm proliferating after the Second World War in country areas where there were no cinemas, enjoying a boom until the effects of TV began to bite in the Fifties. To meet the needs of the mobile cinemas—and later the shows on board ships, in aircraft, and other non-theatrical purposes—the major distributors formed 16mm sound libraries which have remained in one form or another ever since.

Since that time, 16mm sound has become all important to TV, not only as an economical and convenient medium for both newsreel and feature production, but also as a means of presenting cinema films on the small screen, TV stations keeping 16mm prints of features for use in their transmissions (although some, like the BBC in Britain, insist on using 35mm wherever possible).

Although in America before the Second World War, 16mm sound features were available to collectors, they were not normally offered on sale in Britain at this time. Yet, even in Britain there are occasionally 16mm sound prints from the Thirties that come to light. Not long ago a friend came across a number of pre-war 16mm sound prints lying long forgotten in the corner of an office cupboard. These were two-reelers typical of their time. One was a short on Hollywood with scenes of stars off duty and a general look around the film capital in the Thirties. Another reel was a movingly directed documentary of life in the New Forest village of Minstead, still unspoilt at the time it was made. And, most interesting of all, there was a well-produced publicity film proclaiming the food value of bread starring the comic with protruding teeth and goofy voice, Claude Dampier, showing that even in advertising the music hall tradition was as much an influence as it was in British comedy films of the Thirties. Maybe a movie such as this is not as exciting as a long lost feature, but in its way every bit as collectable—as a piece of social history.

Obviously, original pre-war 16mm sound prints fall into the same category as films from the Kodascope and Pathéscope libraries. But prints do come to light in the way I have described above and in Part 1, Chapter 2. Most of the collecting of 16mm sound films is done by purchasing modern prints of old—and not so old—movies. From the quality point of view, 16mm prints made correctly by a professional laboratory—usually direct reduction from 35mm negatives—are as near a collector is likely to get to the 35mm original. It should however be realised that the standard of recent Super 8 prints is completely adequate for home use; it is only for shows in halls to large audiences that 16mm is really essential.

Where there is a 16mm sound copy already in existence, it is easy to make contact duplicates using a process that has appeared in recent years for producing prints relatively cheaply. This is auto-reversal duplicating film—widely used for making film editing work prints—which, unlike earlier reversal duplicating stocks, can be processed simply even by small-time operators. Obviously prints made by this method do not have the quality of direct reductions from 35mm. Reversal prints can be identified by the black rebate they have in the sprocket hole area of the film; copies produced by reduction printing always have clear film in this area. Not surprisingly, this is one of the methods used to produce illicit dupes by film pirates.

Another technique, even cheaper to operate if an illicit "duper" is intent on producing a number of prints for sale, is for him to make a contact negative from a 16mm sound print and from this to run off any number of positives. These dupes, usually having a clear surround in the sprocket hole area, are not readily recognisable as such on a cursory examination. More than likely it will be their degraded quality on the screen that will prove that they are not original prints.

There is no easy way of duplicating colour movies. Printing and processing colour dupes requires more elaborate equipment, more skill on the part of the operator, and uses more expensive film stock than black and white, so that it is beyond the scope of the amateur duper as well as being uneconomic.

The question of the unauthorised duplicating of existing prints raises one of the major problems that has bedevilled 16mm sound collecting in recent years: film piracy. The term "film pirate" has an unpleasant ring to it. Usually a film pirate is considered to be a person who dupes and sells movies without the permission of the copyright owners. And it is these people who have received the attention of the lawyers of the major distributors. But those described as film pirates are often private collectors, the reason being that many collectors tends to trade and sell films surplus to their requirements in common with all collectors (whoever heard of a philatelist who did not trade his surplus stamps?). Even those private collectors who merely want to own and show prints of the Hollywood classics of the Thirties can be prosecuted for being in possession of copyrighted material. In Britain particularly, collectors have had movies confiscated by the police and have faced charges in recent times.

Film piracy is not a new phenomenon. Right back at the movies' infancy, pioneer Sigmund Lubin was noted for his laboratory's ability to make pirate prints from other, more creative producers' work. One victim was Georges Méliès, the French wizard whose ingenious trick films were all the rage around the turn of the century. Seeing their movies being exploited by their unscrupulous rivals, pioneer producers like Méliès resorted to a strange subterfuge to ensure the copyright of their work. This was done by incorporating their company logo in part of the scenery, so that you might see incongruously the American Biograph "AB" symbol popping up on the headboard of the heroine's death-bed, or the Edison "E" hanging on a castle wall behind a couple of fencing swashbucklers! At that time the law was clear about the illegality of copying a trade mark but hazy about the copyright of movie images. Needless to say, even these ruses did not deter the dedicated film duper.

The pirating of 16mm movies seems to have been founded in the period of the Second World War when the prints made for entertaining the troops found their way into collectors' hands. Today, an obvious source for the film duper are the prints in circulation to TV studios which can be "borrowed" or go astray while the duper uses them to produce negatives for illegal printing. In addition to illegal dupes there are of course other "tricky" prints floating around, from a variety of sources.

Probably the reason for the recent spasmodic attempts by the major distributors to clamp down on 16mm sound collectors is not because of bootleg prints of old black-and-white movies of the Thirties and Forties, but because prints of current releases have found their way into collectors' hands. Some dyed-in-the-wool collectors are not content with the "golden oldies". They like to have the very latest films to show, treating it as a challenge that they should own copies of them. This has enraged some distributors who have initiated "film hunts" to track down both the often shady sources of such prints, and the collectors who have them in their private libraries. Unfortunately, the unwitting collector of vintage material has sometimes been caught up in the same net.

If all this were not enough to harass the 16mm sound collector, he is also the prey of con-men, the rip-off racketeers of the collecting scene. As most of the buying of films by collectors in the United States is by mail, unscrupulous dealers sometimes offer subjects for sale, then fail to deliver the goods after they receive the money posted to them. The trouble is that keen collectors, in their anxiety to get certain titles, allow their enthusiasm to overstep their good sense and fail to check carefully the credentials of unknown sources.

Typical of a collector who was swindled is a young movie enthusiast who wrote of his experience to a collectors' magazine (a publication that receives regular reports of similar incidents). He placed an advertisement for a film he wanted in another publication. This was answered by a dealer claiming to have the movie for sale. The collector sent a money order, yet after several months of waiting the film failed to arrive. Eventually he did get a letter from the vendor, still full of promises—but still no film. Finally, his letters were returned "Moved —left no address" . . .

"The Big Reel" (Empire Publishing Inc., Drawer B, Summerfield, North Carolina 27358), a publication concentrating on advertisements placed by 16mm collectors (both sales and wants), insists on two references from would-be advertisers, and offers to investigate complaints by collectors who are cheated. The publishers of this useful magazine also operate an organisation, Collector's Bureau International, which offers a service for collectors, checking on advertising, handling complaints and generally providing information on the film collecting scene.

The legal availability of films on 16mm sound is determined by the law of copyright. In Britain, copyright exists for fifty years from the original release date of the film, though this simple rule can become confused. It may be that the author of the story on which the movie is based can claim his rights, namely the copyright in his literary work, which exists for fifty years after his death, so that his heirs can enjoy the benefit. It takes a long time for creative work to get into the public domain in Britain (for example, the comic operas of Gilbert and Sullivan entered the public domain only recently, fifty years after the death of the librettist, W. S. Gilbert). Consequently, there are no sound films free of copyright restrictions.

In America—at present—copyright protection is obtained for twenty-eight years after the film is registered. At the end of this time, it is possible for the film's owner to re-copyright it for a further twenty-eight years. In practice, the majority—but not all—of the movies made by the major producers of Hollywood's heyday—M.G.M., Paramount, Warner Brothers, 20th Century-Fox, Columbia, and Universal—have been re-copyrighted. This means that many of the sound movies of the Thirties and Forties that are so attractive to the collector are still jealously guarded by their copyright owners. However, despite the entitlement for a second twenty-eight years in copyright, there are many worthwhile sound films not only American, but also British and Conti-, nental titles, that have entered the public domain in the United States (but NOT in Britain) when their copyrights lapsed after the first term.

One copyright anomaly caused a minor sensation in 1976. Inadvertently, M.G.M., a company that guarded its prints so closely that even its directors were not allowed to borrow copies to show in their homes, let one of its classic musicals, *Till the Clouds Roll By* (1946), fall into the public domain, making it one of the most modern major subjects to be outside the protection of copyright. The once great Hollywood studio excused their lapse by saying that with forty subjects a year coming up for re-copyrighting, mistakes could occur. In any case, it had no monetary value!

While the studios may be careless, keen-eyed Super 8 and 16mm distributors are on the look out for movies that fail to get re-copyrighted since it is perfectly legal in the United States to make and sell prints once the copyright has lapsed. And it is in this way that public domain, legal 16mm sound films are available. Other legal 16mm prints are released by certain distributors who have been licensed by the copyright owners (one example is Blackhawk who sell 16mm prints of Laurel and Hardy movies by arrangement with Hal Roach Studios Inc.).

16mm films in the public domain are, of course, available from more than one source since once a movie is out of copyright any distributor who can acquire master material is entitled to make prints for sale. One snag here is that a company without a suitable master could buy a print from another distributor and make a dupe negative from which it can produce its own copies; clearly these will be inferior. There is no way of avoiding this situation, it is just part of the price to be paid when a movie gets into the public domain.

Before reviewing a selection of the important movies to be found on 16mm sound, there are several points worth observing. All the titles mentioned are subjects that are advertised by reputable sources, and are claimed to be legal: either movies that are licensed for sale by the distributors or in the public domain. As I have said, once a movie is in the public domain it may be available from a number of distributors, so the 16mm movies mentioned are not linked to any particular company.

More and more movies that once would have only appeared on 16mm are now being released in parallel on Super 8. In some instances where a title is available in Super 8 as well as 16mm it will be followed by the symbol S8. Similarly you will find reference to 16mm availability in other parts of this book where appropriate, for example in the Collectors' Pieces.

British collectors fare badly in the realms of 16mm sound. Unlike their American colleagues they do not have access to movies in the public domain; so far, there are no sound films old enough to fall into this category. And there are at present no films licensed for sale. A few years ago, there were a few 16mm "package movies" consisting of one-reel extracts from the Astaire-Rogers musicals and *King Kong* for sale, but their distributor—Robert Kingston—no longer handles these subjects. Also in the past there were licensed copies of the Hal Roach Laurel and Hardy and Charley Chase comedies freely available. About the only films the British collector can purchase are the one reel cut-downs from Universal (originally Castle Films) imported from America, but these are hardly enough to sustain a healthy collector's appetite. So for most purposes, 16mm sound collecting in Britain is a non-event. There are a few die-hard collectors who run the gauntlet with bootleg films, but most British collectors have now switched to Super 8 which has so much more to offer.

It is ironic, in view of the non-availability of 16mm sound features for British film buffs, that some of the best public domain titles freely on sale in the United States are British movies. The early films of Alfred Hitchcock are especially well represented. Firstly there is his brilliant talkie debut, *Blackmail* (1929)—see page 188—with its imaginative use of sound, like the moment where the guilt-stricken Annie Ondra hears only the word "knife" in the gossiping chit chat of a nosey neighbour talking about the murder. Then there is the rarely seen *Murder* (1931), again using experimental subjective sound as juryman Herbert Marshall, convinced of the innocence of the girl in the dock, tracks down the real murderer. These two titles were made for BIP; Hitchcock's work became even better when he switched to Gaumont British, which had at the time one of Britain's all-time great producers, Michael Balcon, at the helm. *The Man Who Knew Too Much* (1935) has been the only one of Hitchcock's British thrillers which he has re-made (in 1956) but there is little doubt that the original (on 16mm) is far superior. It may not have Doris Day singing a song hit, but it does have a sharp sense of humour, a splendidly observed gang of conspirators led by Peter Lorre at his best, rivetting suspense when Edna Best's scream in the Albert Hall averts an assassination, and the tense climax of a Sidney Street-like siege when the child Nova Pilbeam is rescued from her kidnappers.

In many ways *The Thirty Nine Steps* (1936)(S8) is the most satisfying of all Hitchcock's British movies. One of his cleverest blends of thrills with a light touch, it has humour springing naturally from its dramatic moments, Robert Donat and Madeleine Carroll making a fine team as the man wrongfully accused of murder and his unwilling helper, with their famous scene when they spend the night handcuffed together in a Scottish hotel bedroom. Significantly, this is the movie that Hitchcock has referred back to most in his Hollywood output. Peter Lorre appeared again for Hitchcock in *The Secret Agent* (1936)(S8) as the curly-haired "Mexican", a paid killer who travels with the British spy Ashenden (John Gielgud), an ironic espionage thriller less well known than the other Hitchcock Gaumont British movies. From 1936, a strong year for the British director, came *Sabotage* (S8), concerning a foreign terrorist (Oscar Homolka) intent on destroying targets in London. Highlighted by the death of the young brother of the saboteur's wife, killed while delivering a movie-can loaded with a time bomb, and the murder of the guilty husband by the grief-stricken woman, this unusually grim thriller has a powerful performance by Sylvia Sidney and some memorable cameo roles like the odious bird fancier (William Dewhurst) who constructs the terrorists' bombs.

Young and Innocent (1937)(S8) continues the favourite Hitchcockian theme of an innocent man on the run from a false murder accusation. This time he's helped by a girl who happens to be the daughter of the chief constable! One of the earliest films to be shot at the then new Pinewood studios in Buckinghamshire, this movie is noted for its *dénouement* which has a lengthy tracking shot across a hotel lounge right up to the drummer in a band, and then to a screen-filling close-up of the impediment that identifies him as the true murderer: twitching eyes!

In 1938, Hitchcock completed *The Lady Vanishes* (S8) another engaging combination of comedy and thrills, surely one of the director's best-ever films. In it, Margaret Lockwood finds that the little old lady (Dame May Whitty) she has met on a transcontinental express has disappeared without trace—and faces a blank wall of disbelief from the other passengers when she tries to find her new friend. With its superb collection of *Grand Hotel*-like cameos, topped by Basil Radford and Naunton Wayne as a couple of true-blue cricket bores who, despite all the sinister goings on around them are only concerned about the latest score, this vastly entertaining movie still wears its years lightly. And with it, Hitchcock's immensely creative Gaumont British period is completed, a series happily available in its entirety to the 16mm sound collector.

While Michael Balcon was producing the Hitchcock movies for Gaumont British, he also handled the work of other directors—particularly good being those of his erstwhile partner Victor Saville. Take, for example, two of his stylish musicals featuring Jessie Matthews (an extremely popular British dancing star who nearly went to Hollywood to partner Fred Astaire—only illness prevented her). *Evergreen* (1934) has a tuneful score by Rodgers and Hart and spectacular dance routines rivalling Berkeley, and *It's Love Again* (1936) has Jessie impersonating a fabulous society figure to help her gossip columnist boy-friend keep his job; catchy music and inventive comedy still come over well in this bright little musical, proving that Balcon's instinct for imaginative entertainment was not confined to the Hitchcock thrillers. The Gaumont British musical style now appears as a splendid evocation of feather-light inconsequence against sets in the Art Deco manner.

In different vein from G.B. are *Dr. Syn* (1938) with grand old man George Arliss as the country vicar who smuggles in his spare time, and *The Clairvoyant* (*The Evil Mind*) (1935) which stars Claude Rains (not long after his "unseen" Hollywood debut in *The Invisible Man*, 1933) as a fake mind reader suddenly discovering he has the power to foretell the future—a neatly-turned melodrama which has the added bonus of an excellent performance by Fay Wray—taking time off from Hollywood encounters with King Kong and wax-masked Lionel Atwill!

Fay Wray also excels in *Bulldog Jack* (1935)(S8), a Gaumont British comedy thriller directed by Walter Forde (Britain's only successful silent comic). Her co-star in this vastly enjoyable spoof of the Bulldog Drummond yarns is Jack Hulbert, of the breezy manner and the prominent jaw. With a lot of the action convincingly set in a disused station on London's Underground and in the British Museum, this well-observed parody succeeds in being more exciting than the movies it is humorously mocking. Ralph Richardson plays a completely nutty villain, gleefully driving a tube train to destruction in a wildly suspenseful climax while Hulbert and his "silly ass" side kick, Algy (his real life brother Claude), check off the stations as they speed towards the final crash!

Fray Wray is also on 16mm in the charming musical she made with debonair song-and-dance man Jack Buchanan while on her stay in England, *When Knights*

Claude Rains as the mind-reader in The Clairvoyant (The Evil Mind)(1935) *and below Fay Wray and Mary Clare in the same film.*

Were Bold (1936), a movie made for an independent company. And, completing the fine range of Gaumont British subjects, there is the touching historical romance with a strong cast headed by Cedric Hardwicke, John Mills and youthful Nova Pilbeam as Lady Jane Grey, *Nine Days a Queen* (1936) concerning the political in-fighting following the Tudor succession and the girl who unwittingly goes to the scaffold.

Other major British movies from the Thirties to be found on 16mm sound are the complete version of *Things to Come* (1936)(S8), produced by Alexander Korda, and also Korda's splendid *Private Life of Henry VIII* (1933), the movie that put British films on the map, and his *Scarlet Pimpernel* (1935) with Leslie Howard perfectly cast as the aristocrat who is a fop by day and a man of action at night, saving victims from the guillotine.

Particularly noteworthy on 16mm are *Dark Journey* (1937)(S8) with a young Vivien Leigh and the ever-impressive Conrad Veidt; *Dinner at the Ritz* (1937) (S8), a stylish whodunnit with David Niven and the French Annabella; *I Stand Condemned* (1936)(originally *Moscow Nights*), directed by Anthony Asquith; and Asquith's finest film, *Pygmalion* (1938), with beautiful performances by Wendy Hiller and Leslie Howard. Howard can also be seen in his final film,

Left, Albert Préjean as the seller of songs in Sous les Toits de Paris (1930).

Below, Peter Lorre and the child killer of M (1931)

Spitfire (*The First of the Few*) (1942), as the designer of the famous fighter plane of the Second World War, a film which he directed not long before his tragic death in an air crash.

Probably because they were considered to have little commercial value for theatrical reissue, some movies from the Continent, like the British titles, were never re-copyrighted after twenty-eight years and have fallen into the public domain. But this in no way diminishes their value for collectors; there are a number of important subjects from Europe, many considered classics by any standard, readily available on 16mm sound.

There are Eisenstein's two sound masterpieces: *Alexander Nevsky* (1939(S8) with its incredible battle on the ice and Prokofiev's stirring score, and the monumental *Ivan the Terrible* (Part I and II) (1944–46), part II complete with its colour sequence. From Germany there is Fritz Lang's *M* (1931)—Peter Lorre astonishing in his screen debut as the pathetic child murderer—and Marlene Dietrich in full flower as the provocative Lola in von Sternberg's summation of expressionist movie making, *The Blue Angel* (1930), plus what is the greatest film ever to be directed by a woman: *Olympische Spiele* (1936), Leni Riefenstahl's stunning documentary.

Some of the finest works of the French cinema of the Thirties and Forties are to be found on 16mm. Jean Cocteau's quirkily eccentric but fascinating *Blood of a Poet* (1932) is one of the earliest sound subjects. Even better are the two delightful semi-musicals from René Clair, both pointing the way to witty, imaginative uses of sound: *Sous les Toits de Paris* (1930), with Albert Préjean singing the most evocative of theme songs, and *Le Million* (1930), with its crazy hunt for a lost lottery ticket. Clair's *A Nous la Liberté* (1931), most satirical of all this distinguished director's thoughtful comedies, is often said to have been the mainspring of Chaplin's *Modern Times*. Like the other French classics, it is available on 16mm with subtitles.

Representing the work of Jean Renoir, one of the finest of all directors, is *Boudu Sauvé des Eaux* (1932), with Michel Simon as the rebellious tramp saved by a bourgeois bookseller; *Les Bas Fonds* (*The Lower Depths*) (1936), Louis Jouvet excelling in this version of a Maxim Gorky story; *La Grande Illusion* (1938), one of the truly great movies of all time with Erich von Stroheim and Jean Gabin at the peak of their acting powers; and *Règle du Jeu* (*The Rules of the Game*) (1939)(S8), a constant candidate for the ten best movies ever made.

From Julien Duvivier comes *Pépé Le Moko* (1936), with Jean Gabin as the petty crook of the title. This movie so attracted Hollywood that it was reproduced almost exactly frame for frame as *Algiers* (1938)(S8, also on 16mm) with Charles Boyer in Gabin's role (which brought to the screen: "Come with me to the Casbah"—an essential part of every mimic's stock in trade.) Co-starring with Boyer and making her American debut was Hedy Lamarr, already famous after appearing in the nude in the Czech movie *Ekstase* (1933)(S8, also on 16mm). One of Duvivier's later works, *Panique* (1947), has Michel Simon as an eccentric framed in a near perfect murder plot and is based on a powerful Simenon thriller.

Three other important subjects on 16mm make up this cross-section of French cinema: *La Kermesse Héroïque* (*Carnival in Flanders*) (1936), Jacques Feyder's beautifully designed and photographed comedy of the Flemish women who disregard their cowardly husbands to welcome the Spanish invaders of their town; Marcel Carné's *Le Jour Se Lève* (1939), Jean Gabin again as a petty crook trapped by police in a gaunt house and re-living—in flashback— the events of his downfall, summing up several pessimistic movies scripted by Jacques Prévert; and, finally, Henri-Georges Clouzot's suspense thriller made during the Occupation, *Le Corbeau* (*The Raven*) (1943), about a poison pen letter writer undermining a whole community.

It would be foolish to pretend that the range of American sound movies in the public domain—and hence legally available on 16mm—is more than a small fraction of the output of what were Hollywood's most productive years. The American titles that are legal on 16mm are a curiously mixed selection, largely because they have fallen into the public domain by oversight rather than by any conscious plan. Some of the subjects are of considerable interest, while others— like the B westerns, for example—are of more specialised appeal. Nevertheless, there is still plenty to grab the attention of all keen collectors.

Pierre Fresnay and Erich von Stroheim in Renoir's La Grande Illusion (1937).

When the good guys wore white! Ken Maynard is the B Western hero found in many 16mm collections.

There are many American subjects from the early days of the talkies, 1928 to 1933—the period when directors and actors were coming to terms with the new medium, a fascinating era of rapid change and experiment which the collector is able to study in detail. The earliest of the sound films available is a print of a movie made in England with the pioneer DeForest Phonofilm system. (DeForest was the inventor of the radio tube as well as the first successful sound -on-film process). This is a short, *Mr. Smith Wakes Up* (1926), starring a young Elsa Lanchester. One of the earliest sound features is *The Great Gabbo* (1929), which although not a horror movie is an attempt at a theme that has provided the basis for several sinister thrillers: a ventriloquist (strongly played by Erich von Stroheim) is only able to express himself through his dummy. Directed by one of Hollywood's best silent movie makers, James Cruze, it blends its drama with "camp" musical numbers, including a weird dance routine of a spider catching a fly in its web.

There is the first—and last—attempt by the "master", D. W. Griffith, at a major sound film: *Abraham Lincoln* (1930). Held in little regard on its first release, it is now looked at more sympathetically. And there are some of the earliest sound cartoons made in the wake of the astonishing success of Disney's talkie Mickey Mouse, like the inventive animated cartoons of Paul Terry, Ub Iwerks with his character Flip the Frog (after his split with Disney), and Max Fleischer—all offering a different angle on how to combine sound with picture.

The vintage movie musical is revived in the bland style of *Vagabond Lover*, starring Rudy Vallee, the original "crooner," with pretty Sally Blane (sister of the better known Loretta Young): "the king of song has one facial expression", commented "Photoplay" tartly on this first talkie appearance by heartthrob Vallee. Another unusual musical is *Reaching for the Moon* (1931), written by Irving Berlin but with only one song—crooned by Bing Crosby. It stars Douglas Fairbanks, with some of his original acrobatic sparkle, as a playboy who wins and loses a fortune in the Depression. Supported by Bebe Daniels (blonde instead of brunette) and Edward Everett Horton, one of the most accomplished character comedians and master of the "double take" as his valet, this a decidedly collectable rarity. Fairbanks is also on 16mm in *Around the World in Eighty Minutes* (1931), more a travelogue than a story film.

Norma Talmadge, outstanding as a silent artiste, stars on 16mm as *Dubarry* (1930). Norma unfortunately had a strong Brooklyn accent, totally unsuited to the romantic costume roles she favoured, and was an early casualty of the talkie revolution. While some well-established silent screen careers were destroyed by the microphone, the 16mm lists have many titles featuring stars soon to become famous through the talkies. There's *The Last Mile* (1932)(S8) with Clark Gable in a bit part; *Hell House* (1932)(S8), Bette Davis partnering fast-talking Pat O'Brien; Ginger Rogers starring in a murder mystery, *Shriek in the Night* (1933); Jean Arthur and Robert Armstrong in *Dangerous Lights* (1930)—a railroad melodrama; and dependable Joan Blondell as one of *Three Broadway Girls* (1932), first of many attempts at the theme of three gold-diggers looking for rich husbands.

Major directors' early sound films are also well covered. Subjects include King Vidor's *Street Scene* (1932), a successful stage to screen adaptation of Elmer Rice's powerful play on New York's tenement life with a memorable—and oft repeated—score by Alfred Newman; Vidor's *Bird of Paradise* (1932), with Joel McCrea and Dolores Del Rio complete with a dance routine devised by Busby Berkeley; Lewis Milestone's *The Front Page* (1931) and his version of Somerset Maugham's *Rain* (1932)(S8) with Joan Crawford scoring as the prostitute who seduces a clergyman. And there's the minor horror movie that has earned classic status for its economically told story and its understated terrors: *The Most Dangerous Game* (1932)(S8) made on the same sets as *King Kong* with *Kong's* Fay Wray and Robert Armstrong, and co-directed by Ernest Schoedsack (*Kong's* co-director) with Irving Pichel. Irving Pichel's attempt at making an A movie for B picture producer Monogram in 1933, *Oliver Twist*, is also on 16mm

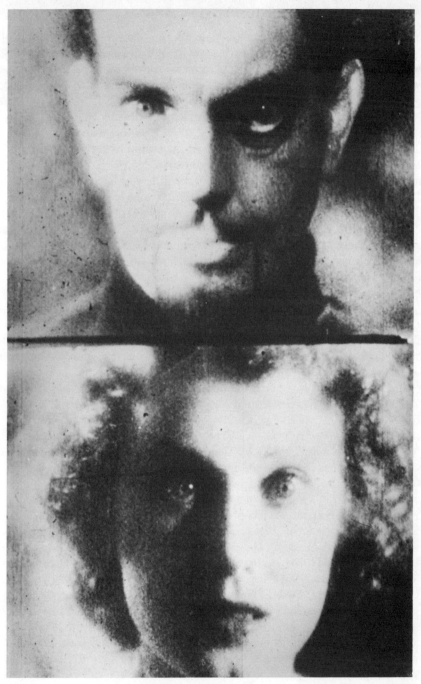

Fay Wray at the mercy of Leslie Banks's mad Count Zaroff in The Most Dangerous Game (The Hounds of Zaroff)(1932) *(adjacent frames from a 16mm print).*

(Dickie Moore, an ex-Our Gang graduate, playing the winsome orphan) while, from a major studio, there's the early sound movie *Svengali* (1931), directed by Archie Mayo with some astonishing camerawork by Barney McGill and expressionistic settings by Anton Grot, John Barrymore giving a full-blooded portrayal of the evil hypnotist.

With the solving of the technical problems of the talkies (faults like static cinematography and noisy sound tracks), there was the evolving of a style of production combining the best elements of the silent movies with the narrative advantages of sound. Hollywood began to reel off an ever increasing number of movies with a good proportion of memorable titles—it had reached its Golden Age! Some of the most interesting 16mm subjects come from this era.

Here are some worthwhile titles to be found. William Wellman's *A Star Is Born* (1937, in my view superior to the overrated Judy Garland re-make), starring Janet Gaynor and Fredric March in peak form, is available as a colour copy from a Technicolor print, as is Wellman's "crazy comedy," *Nothing Sacred* (1937), from Ben Hecht's witty screenplay, which has Carole Lombard as the girl with supposedly only a few weeks to live and Fredric March as the unscrupulous reporter who makes a nationwide heroine of her. King Vidor's worthy *Our Daily Bread* (1934), a documentary-like look at the life of one American farmer and his family, spoilt by weak acting but notable for its final irrigation sequence, is yet another work by this major—but uneven—director on 16mm, while John Ford's *Judge Priest* (1934) looks at the rural character Ford was to return to later, here played by the inimitable Will Rogers.

From the Thirties come three classic documentaries on 16mm: *Land Without Bread* (1932), Luis Buñuel's unflinching look at poverty in a country region in Spain; Joris Ivens' *New Earth* (1931-34) on the reclamation of the Zuyder Zee, with a stunning musical score by Hans Eisler; and the GPO Film Unit's best-known movie, beautifully capturing the magic of steam railways, *Night Mail* (1936)(S8), directed by Basil Wright with Harry Watt.

Oddities from the period include *Crimson Romance* (1934)—with Ben Lyon and Erich von Stroheim (who preferred to disown his performance) in what amounts to a re-run of *Hell's Angels* fleshed out with out-takes from the original aerial epic made by Howard Hughes. There are also interesting shorts like *La Cucuracha* (1934), the first live-action film to be made by the three-colour Technicolor process; Bob Hope's first movie, *Going Spanish* (1934); and, particularly intriguing, Orson Welles' first film, a six-minute-long amateur experimental movie, *Hearts of Age* (1934), in which he plays a grotesque illusionist and already displays an interest in unusual camera angles and lighting.

Many 16mm releases come from independent producers so we find, for example, two enjoyable features from the short-lived Grand National outfit, starring James Cagney after he had a tiff over his contract with Warner Brothers. These are *Something to Sing About* (1937)(S8), one of Cagney's infrequent musicals with him as a song and dance man crashing into Hollywood, and

Great Guy (1936)(S8) with Jimmy as a tough weights-and-measures inspector cleaning up a racket in the meat business in the same way he had operated in *G–Men*.

From the range of titles that have slipped through the copyright net into the public domain there are *They Made Me a Criminal* (1939)(S8), starring John Garfield as a boxer who thinks he has killed his opponent, hiding out in the country with the Dead End Kids—an unusual subject to have been directed by Busby Berkeley; Shirley Temple as *The Little Princess* (1939)(S8), one of the astonishing little star's few colour movies; a spectacular from Warner Brothers, *The Santa Fe Trail* (1940)(S8), complete with Michael Curtiz's direction, Max Steiner's score, and Errol Flynn and Olivia de Havilland; Alexander Korda's fine version of Kipling's *Jungle Book* (1940)(S8), starring the likable Indian boy Sabu as Mowgli of the wolves; and Capra's powerful *Meet John Doe* (1941)(S8) with Gary Cooper and Barbara Stanwyck, a typical Capra social comment, full of his touches, about a nice guy exploited by crooked politicians.

Another selection of movies from the major studios that have legally reached 16mm (and Super 8, too, for that matter) are certain series "packages" that have been licensed for sale for home use. So we find Paramount's lively Bulldog Drummond series which had Ray Milland as the man of action in *Bulldog Drummond Escapes* (1937)(S8) followed by John Howard as Sapper's fictional hero in *Bulldog Drummond Comes Back* (1937)(S8) which also had John Barrymore as Colonel Nielsen of Scotland Yard indulging his penchant for disguise in what is one of the best of the series. Howard starred in several Drummond titles including *Bulldog Drummond's Secret Police* (1939)(S8), notable for its tense atmospheric climax in a sinister castle complete with secret tunnels and a torture chamber.

A further group of movies to reach 16mm, oddly enough also detective stories, are the up-dated Sherlock Holmes subjects made by Universal in the Forties. Starring the screen's definitive Holmes and Watson, Basil Rathbone and Nigel Bruce, the stories in this curious but enjoyable series were initially based on Conan Doyle's original plots with first class players in support, like Lionel Atwill (*Sherlock Holmes and the Secret Weapon*—1942—S8). Later, the modernised Victorian sleuth has to contend with such comic characters as the grotesque Spider Woman (*The Spider Woman*—1944—S8), played by a fine actress worthy of better roles, Gale Sondergaard, and the exploitation of the facially deformed Rondo Hatton as the Creeper in *The Pearl of Death* (1944)(S8).

Major titles from the Forties legally available on 16mm include a couple of essentially wartime subjects. *This is the Army* (1943)(S8), the movie version of Irving Berlin's all soldier show with a roster of Warner Brothers contract players directed by Michael Curtiz, and *Stage Door Canteen* (1943)(S8), a lavish variety show with numerous guest star appearances.

Movies of greater merit include *Scarlet Street* (1946), Fritz Lang's bitter thriller with Edward G. Robinson as a weekend artist whose life is destroyed by a scheming tart (Joan Bennett); Lewis Milestone's powerful war story of an attack on a German hide-out in Italy, *A Walk in the Sun* (1946), starring Dana Andrews and Richard Conte; Jean Renoir's best American film, *The Southerner* (1945), about a poor farmer and his battles with natural disaster; Orson Welles' *The Stranger* (1946)(S8), Welles as a Nazi war criminal taking a new identity as a university professor only to be tracked down by Government agent Edward G. Robinson and ending up skewered on the sword of a statue; and the interesting —but ultimately disappointing—combination of Preston Sturges and Harold Lloyd, *The Sin of Harold Diddlebock* (1946)(S8), in which Sturges tried to bring up to date the character Lloyd played in his silent, *The Freshman* (1927), but only proved how much better the young Harold was in the original (seen at the beginning of this version).

From the later Forties just before the time when the twenty-eight year copyright period still appli s comes *Life with Father* (1947)(S8) in colour, directed by Michael Curtiz, with William Powell excelling as the authoritarian father who finds he is not really in control of his wife and sons, and the M-G-M copyright slip-up, *Till the Clouds Roll By* (1946)(S8), remembered for Judy Garland's singing of "Look for the Silver Lining" and some good numbers by Frank Sinatra, Kathryn Grayson, Lena Horne and other M-G-M contractees in a revue type biopic on Jerome Kern hardly in the same class as the winning streak of M-G-M musicals that were to follow later.

So the archive of 16mm movies goes on. And yet—as I have already indicated—many of the best subjects are also on Super 8. In addition, most major Hollywood producers are starting to issue legal Super 8 prints of some of the favourite titles in their vaults, which although in the form of twenty minute digests are very expertly edited to retain the story-line and the best loved scenes. In the face of this competition and the legal problems that bedevil 16mm collecting, it is not surprising that, more and more, Super 8 is the dominant gauge for both distributors and collectors.

The films mentioned in this chapter are released by the following companies, whose addresses can be found in the directory at the end of this book: Blackhawk Films, Griggs Moviedrome, Hollywood Film Exchange, Niles Film Products Inc., Reel Images Inc., Select Film Library Inc., and Thunderbird Films.

Part Seven

Into the Future

What will the future hold for film collecting? What is likely to be the outcome of current trends? In the introduction, the use of electronic techniques—like video-tape and video-disc—for the presentation of old movies was briefly mentioned. But although mass produced video recordings will soon be perfected, there is little doubt that they will appeal to a less committed public than truly keen film collectors. The purchase of this kind of soft-ware will probably fall into the same category as the casual buying of the current musical top of the pops.

Certainly electronic recordings will have none of the lure of original old movie prints. Their vintage photographic quality, and the fact that they are antiques, in the best sense of the word, gives early sprocketed films their special mystique. Even though modern Super 8 reprints are often generations removed from the originals, they are still on sprocketed film and from the collectors' viewpoint have some association with the real cinema. So it seems probable that film prints will be appearing for Super 8 collectors for many years to come.

There is no doubt that Super 8 has finally become the prime collectors' gauge. In the past couple of years, a clamp-down by major film companies on the circulation of pirated 16mm prints has led many collectors of the larger gauge to turn to Super 8 as an outlet for their hobby. Setting the trend for the future has been the rapid expansion of Super 8 sound, already creating a revolution on the collecting scene. With increasing numbers of Super 8 sound projectors in domestic use, bought initially to project the movies shot on direct recording sound cameras, a new market for Super 8 sound releases has opened up and enterprising distributors are looking for business there. One less agreeable trend resulting from the growth of Super 8 sound could be the cutting back of the number of silent prints available.

With so much material appearing in a short space of time, keen collectors should take steps to ensure that the movies being offered to them are satisfactory. They are recommended to complain to distributors and dealers when a print supplied to them fails to meet a reasonable standard of quality. Standards of printing vary enormously. Prints of high and low quality will often appear from the same master of a popular film, with the poor copies occasionally slipping through the net. No reputable distributor will fail to take action over an inferior print returned to him.

Collectors are also advised to make their preferences known to distributors. Strangely enough, many distributors are not really film buffs and the choice of the subjects that they handle is often decided on their own likes and dislikes rather than by market research or a true feeling for the scope of the cinema. The results can be disconcerting. In Britain, dull programmers and modern TV spin-offs are sometimes selected from notable production backlogs, instead of movies of merit both as entertainment and as collectors' items.

Finally, what of the future of possibly the most important of all the factors affecting film collecting—the question of the availability and legality of movies? It is essential that the accepted classics of the screen—silent and sound— should be available for collectors and students to study and enjoy in the privacy of their own homes without the fear of prosecution. While there is every sympathy with a production company whose movies on current theatrical release are getting publicly shown to paying audiences via pirated prints, few collectors have friendly feelings towards the dog in the manger attitude of some copyright owners who prevent the sound classics of the Thirties—or even silent classics of the Twenties in some cases—from being made available for sale for strictly private showing. Some copyright owners would rather destroy irreplaceable movies than see them fall into private collectors' hands. So some way must surely be found whereby legitimate private collectors can own reprints of these much loved classics.

For all the disappointments and frustrations in the range of subjects available for collectors, there are probably more titles to be found currently on release on Super 8 than ever before in the history of narrow gauge movies. With more distributors entering the field and more major distributors taking the newest of the gauges seriously, the future looks promising. And if that is not enough to stimulate the collecting instinct, there is always that moment of moments when a rusty old can in a loft or a junk shop yields up its secrets. It is the dream of incidents like this that gives the real zest and excitement to film collecting.

Postscript

Things are moving fast on the movie collecting scene. Already, during the writing of this book, there have been major developments. These have all been on Super 8, since Standard 8 has now become a gauge of the past in the same way as 9.5mm. With technical improvements on Super 8 projectors, particularly in the sound department, even 16mm is facing significant competition, especially for shows in the home and in smaller halls.

But the real reason for this postscript is to briefly survey the exciting – and ever growing number – of new subjects on the most popular of the gauges. In Britain, Walton have released the Carol Reed classic, *The Third Man* (1950), famed for Anton Karas' haunting zither and Orson Welles' memorable Harry Lime, in both feature-length and digest versions. Mountain Films are now fully involved with their programme of RKO Radio features. *Citizen Kane* (1940) and *King Kong* (1933) have appeared in un-cut feature-length versions, while *Top Hat* (1935) has been issued as a slightly abridged feature. The climactic Empire State Building slaughter of poor old Kong, and Fred and Ginger's interpretations of Irving Berlin's standards in *Top Hat*, have all appeared as shorts. For connoisseurs, the realease of Mark Robson's tense and exciting *The Ghost Ship* (1943), made by Val Lewton's celebrated unit at RKO with Richard Dix excellent as a psychopathic ship's captain, is another welcome addition.

Powell Films have released uncut versions of Launder and Gilliat's immensely enjoyable *The Happiest Days of Your Life* (1950) with the inspired co-starring of Alastair Sim and Margaret Rutherford as warring school heads, and David Lean's well-meaning but dull paean to aircraft, *The Sound Barrier* (1952), as well as his splendid *Hobson's Choice* (1954) with Charles Laughton in one of his finest performances as the boozy bootmaker hoodwinked by his timid – though shrewd – assistant (played impeccably by John Mills). Powell have released in colour the charming *The Railway Children* (1970), the pleasing directorial debut of character comedian Lionel Jeffries.

On the silent side, Breakspear have increased their range of finely printed collectors' items with *The Helpful Sisterhood* (1914) in which Norma Talmadge – not to be seen in many collectors' films – proves her outstanding acting skill as a poor college girl who tries to keep up with the smart set. And there is the long forgotten comedienne Billy Rhodes in the Mutual one reeler, *A Maid to Order* (1918). Perry's Movies have converted some of their silent shorts – and a two reel digest of *The Lost World* (1925) – to sound with musical backing played on the piano. Perry's other silent additions include *Monty's Hair Raising Train Rescue* (a version of Monty Banks' masterpiece *Play Safe*), *Ten Minute Egg* (1925) with Charley Chase, and the ever popular Snub Pollard classic *It's a Gift*.

The Collectors' Club, a British organisation originally concerned with reprints of familiar silent titles sold on a subscription basis like a book-of-the-month club, is now releasing sound shorts. Among the interesting titles released are *Hollywood on Parade*, one of a series from the early Thirties that featured sequences both staged and off the cuff with famous stars of the time, and a Flip the Frog cartoon *The Music Lesson* (1930), animated by the creator of Mickey Mouse, Ub Iwerks, during a temporary break with Disney. Derann Films have negotiated to release on Super 8 the famous Ealing Studios movies. Titles promised are *The Titfield Thunderbolt* (1953), *Dead of Night* (1945), a classic of the macabre – and the archetypal Ealing comedy, *The Lavender Hill Mob* (1950), with Alec Guinness as the timid bank clerk who takes to crime. Already on release are *The Cruel Sea* (1953) with Jack Hawkins in his finest role, and *The Ghost of St. Michael's*, Ealing's continuation of the seedy career of Will Hay's schoolmaster.

In America, Niles have had a scoop with *Hollywood – The Selznick Years*, consisting of extracts from many of the great producer's most famous films including a ten minute segment from *Gone with the Wind* (complete with rare footage of the screen tests to find the right actress to play Scarlett O'Hara). Another batch of collectable titles exclusive to Niles is the complete set of Sherlock Holmes features made by Basil Rathbone and Nigel Bruce (the screen's definitive Holmes and Watson) for Universal. Although awkwardly updated to the Forties (when they were made), they are still great fun.

Milestone Movies have started to convert many titles previously only available from them on Standard 8 to Super 8. They have also started to issue Super 8 sound prints. Two intriguing titles herald their entry into talkies: *The Most Dangerous Game* (1932), the splendid little horror movie that was made concurrently with *King Kong* using many of the same sets and two of Kong's cast: Fay Wray and Robert Armstrong; and Michael Curtiz in top imaginative form in his speedy direction of *The Kennel Murder Case* (1933) – with William Powell starring as the debonair Philo Vance and a strong cast of suspects.

An important breakthrough for Super 8 has been the long-awaited release of several of Sir Charles Chaplin's most famous features (in their full length): *The Gold Rush* (the 1942 sound reissue of the 1925 silent), *The Circus* (1928), *Modern Times* (1936) and *A King in New York* (1957), together with the rarely seen First National Shorts: *A Day's Pleasure* (1919) and *Pay Day* (1922). The pre-print material for these Super 8 prints has been made from Chaplin's 35mm master negatives to give the best possible quality. Somewhat unusually, the Super 8 prints are to be sold on lease and have to be returned to the copyright holder on its expiry.

Yet another great silent comedian's work is being made available for sale. Harlod Lloyd's shorts and features of the Twenties, for so long unseen, are being issued by Time-Life Multimedia in the form of "programmes", either as 16mm prints or as video tape cassettes. So far there appear to be no plans for their Super 8 release.

With a change of title to Universal 8, the long established Castle Films organisation has started to issue 400 ft versions of titles that hitherto have only appeared as rather inadequate one reelers. *The Invisible Man* (1933), *Dracula* (1930), *Frankenstein* (1931) and *The Bride of Frankenstein* (1935) have all been re-edited and re-issued in the longer format. The clever editing of these longer digests conveys very successfully the story-line and flavour of the originals. Similar treatment has been given to more up to date titles like *Thoroughly Modern Millie* (1967) and *Airport* (1969) with this new policy, together with prints of generally excellent quality. It looks as though this Super 8 outlet for the productions of Hollywood's longest established studio is going to provide a wealth of material for collectors.

Columbia is now issuing digests of some of the later Warner Brothers' productions in which they have the rights; other major Hollywood producers are said to be contemplating entering the Super 8 market . . . and so it goes on. Exciting things are happening on the Super 8 scene – things look bright for the future!

Directory of Sources

The code which appears against each distributor's name is used in the Index to identify the original source and the present day availability – where applicable – of the movies discussed in the text.

Companies no longer releasing films

28mm, 17.5mm and 9.5mm

P   Pathescope, Great Britain; Pathe Baby, France; Pathex, U.S.A.
N   Novascope, Great Britain.

Standard 8mm and 16mm

B   Bell and Howell, U.S.A.
E   Ensign Library, Great Britain.
K   Kodascope Library, U.S.A. and Great Britain.
W   Wallace Heaton, Great Britain.
Wy Williams and Ivey, Great Britain.
Un United Artists (UA8)

Some current distributors of Standard 8, Super 8, and 16mm movies for sale to collectors

Great Britain

Br Breakspear Films, 66 Derby Street, Leek, Staffs, ST13 5AJ.
C   Capitol Film Distributors Ltd., 193 Wardour Street, London, WIE 6JZ. (British distributor of Castle – Universal 8 – movies).
D   DCR Films (I of W) Ltd., 94 Avenue Road, Sandown I.o.W.
Dn Derann Film Services, 171 Stourbridge Road, Dudley, West Midlands, DY1 2EQ.
Dy Walt Disney Productions Ltd., 83 Pall Mall, London, SWIY 5EX.
F   Fletcher Films Ltd., 59 The Causeway, Potters Bar, Herts.
M   Mountain Films Ltd., West Central Street, London WC1. (British distributors of Columbia, Ken, and RKO Radio movies).
Py Perry's Movies Ltd., 129 Kingston Road, London SW19 1LU.
Pm P M Films, 39 Windsor End, Beaconsfield, Bucks, HP9 2JN.
Pl Powell Film Distributors Ltd., 6 Hermitage Parade, High Street, Ascot, Berks.

Wn Walton Sound and Film Services Ltd., 87 Richford Street, London, W6 7HN.

U.S.A.

Bk Blackhawk Films 1235 West 5th Street, Davenport, Iowa 52808 (Blackhawk movies are available in Great Britain from Regent Films, 2 Palladium Buildings, Waterloo Road, Blackpool, Lancs.)

C Castle, see Universal 8.

Ct Cinema Eight, Middlesex Avenue, Chester, Connecticut 06412.

Co Columbia Pictures, 8mm Division, 711 Fifth Avenue, New York, NY 10022.

Dy Walt Disney Home Movies, PO Box 407, Paramount, California 90723.

G Griggs Moviedrome – Essex, 263 Harrison Street, Nutley, New Jersey 07110.

I Images, 2 Purdy Avenue, Rye, NY 10580.

Iy Ivy Films, Suite 414CC, 165 West 46th Street, New York, NY 10036.

K Ken Films Inc., 560 Main Street, Fort Lee, New Jersey 07024.

Mi Milestone Movies Corporation, 212 Shelton Road, Monroe, Connecticut 06468.

Ni Niles Film Products Inc., 1141 Mishawaka Avenue, South Bend, Indiana 46615.

S Select Film Library Inc., 115 West 31st Street, New York, NY10001 (This company distributes movies from many of the sources listed.)

T Thunderbird Films, PO Box 65157, Los Angeles, California 900651.

U Universal 8 – originally Castle Films, 404 Park Ave. South, New York, NY 10016.

Germany

A Atlas, now Piccolo Film, Am Michaelianger 1, 8042 Oberschleissheim. (Piccolo movies are available in Great Britain from Mirage Films, Delphi, The Street, Swallowfield, Reading, Berks.)

To confirm the current source of a film, collectors are advised to obtain up to date catalogues from the distributors. For various reasons – the expiry of rights, withdrawal of titles owing to a lack of interest, or even the printing master becoming worn or damaged – the current availability is likely to change.

Index